Upaniṣad Series : 2

Kenopaniṣad

(with text in Sanskrit along with Transliteration,
word-to-word meaning
and an elaborate commentary with
quotations from Śaṅkara Bhāṣya)

Swami Dayananda Saraswati
Arsha Vidya

Arsha Vidya
Research and Publication Trust
Chennai

Published by :
Arsha Vidya Research
and Publication Trust
32 / 4 ' Sri Nidhi ' Apts III Floor
Sir Desika Road Mylapore
Chennai 600 004 INDIA
Tel : 044 2499 7023
Telefax: 2499 7131
Email : avrandpc@gmail.com

ISBN : 978 – 81 – 906059 – 2 – 2

First Edition :	October	2008	Copies : 2000
1st Reprint :	November	2009	Copies : 2000

Design :
Suchi Ebrahim

Printed by :
Sudarsan Graphics
27, Neelakanta Mehta Street
T. Nagar, Chennai 600 017
Email : info@sudarsan.com

CONTENTS

Chapter 3

Chapter 4

PREFACE

I am very happy that the 'Kenopaniṣad' is being brought out in a book-form. I did go through the edited transcript with a pen in hand and I did cross many a 't' and dot a few 'i's.

Though the transcripts were of my classroom lectures given quite a few years back, I was happy to see that I did not have to change anything much in content, much less in the method of teaching. I congratulate the publication team of Smt. Sheela Balaji, headed by Ms. K. Chandra, for their dedicated *sevā*. I am very happy that we have the able services of Sri. Swami Sakshatkritananda and Dr. Martha Doherty. I look forward to many more books, even though they would keep me more busy.

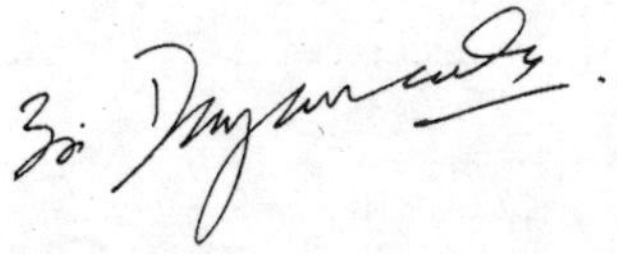

Swami Dayananda Saraswati
September 04 2008

Key to Transliteration and Pronunciation of Sanskrit Letters

Sanskrit is a highly phonetic language and hence accuracy in articulation of the letters is important. For those unfamiliar with the *Devanāgari* script, the international transliteration is a guide to the proper pronunciation of Sanskrit letters.

अ	*a*	*(but)*
आ	*ā*	*(father)*
इ	*i*	*(it)*
ई	*ī*	*(beat)*
उ	*u*	*(full)*
ऊ	*ū*	*(pool)*
ऋ	*ṛ*	*(rhythm)*
ॠ	*ṝ*	*(marine)*
ऌ	*ḷ*	*(revelry)*
ए	*e*	*(play)*
ऐ	*ai*	*(aisle)*
ओ	*o*	*(go)*
औ	*au*	*(loud)*
क	*ka*	*(seek)* 1
ख	*kha*	*(blockhead)**1
ग	*ga*	*(get)* 1
घ	*gha*	*(log house)**1
ङ	*ṅa*	*(sing)* 1
च	*ca*	*(chunk)* 2
छ	*cha*	*(catch him)**2
ज	*ja*	*(jump)* 2
झ	*jha*	*(hedgehog)**2
ञ	*ña*	*(bunch)* 2
ट	*ṭa*	*(true)**3
ठ	*ṭha*	*(anthill)**3
ड	*ḍa*	*(drum)**3
ढ	*ḍha*	*(godhead)**3
ण	*ṇa*	*(under)**3
त	*ta*	*(path)**4
थ	*tha*	*(thunder)**4
द	*da*	*(that)**4
ध	*dha*	*(breathe)**4
न	*na*	*(nut)**4
प	*pa*	*(put)* 5
फ	*pha*	*(loophole)**5
ब	*ba*	*(bin)* 5
भ	*bha*	*(abhor)**5
म	*ma*	*(much)* 5
य	*ya*	*(loyal)*
र	*ra*	*(red)*
ल	*la*	*(luck)*
व	*va*	*(vase)*
श	*śa*	*(sure)*
ष	*ṣa*	*(shun)*
स	*sa*	*(so)*
ह	*ha*	*(hum)*

ं	*ṁ*	*anusvāra*	(nasalisation of preceding vowel)
:	*ḥ*	*visarga*	(aspiration of preceding vowel)
*			No exact English equivalents for these letters

1.	Guttural	–	Pronounced from throat
2.	Palatal	–	Pronounced from palate
3.	Lingual	–	Pronounced from cerebrum
4.	Dental	–	Pronounced from teeth
5.	Labial	–	Pronounced from lips

The 5th letter of each of the above class – called nasals – are also pronounced nasally.

INTRODUCTION

The source book for self-knowledge is the Veda in general and Vedanta in particular. The whole Veda is looked upon as a means of knowledge. What is counted as a separate means of knowledge must have a subject matter of its own; it must not be available for any other means of knowledge. We count the sense organs backed by the mind as a separate means of knowledge because what is achieved by them cannot be achieved by any other means. If it can be achieved by some other means, then the senses are not a separate means of knowledge. So, perception, *pratyakṣa,* which is five-fold is counted as one means of knowledge. This is five-fold because within perception itself we see each sense organ having its own sphere of operation. The eyes have access to colours and forms; ears have access to sound and so on. What is accomplished by a given sense organ is not accomplished by others, which is why we count each sense organ as a distinct *pramāṇa,* means of knowledge.

This is so because it causes *pramā,* knowledge. *Mā* means knowledge. *Pra* is an *upasarga,* a prefix to *mā*. *Pramāyāḥ karaṇa-bhūtatvāt,* being in the form of *karaṇa,* the means for *pramā,* the sense organs are called *pramāṇa*s. The five sense organs objectify the world directly, and therefore we call them, collectively, *pratyakṣa-pramāṇa,* direct means of knowledge.

This is also called *mūla-pramāṇa,* the source of all means of knowledge. For instance, the Veda is a means of knowledge that is outside this perception, but the words of the Veda have to be received by one's ears or they have to be read by one's eyes. Denied of visual and auditory perception, there is no way of knowing the Vedas. The *pratyakṣa-pramāṇa* is, therefore, a very important means in gaining any knowledge. In fact, the other means of knowledge depend upon *pratyakṣa-pramāṇa* for their operation.

Some schools of thought accept only *pratyakṣa* as a means of knowledge, which is why counting the number is important here. Any view held, based on the number of *pramāṇa*s accepted, creates a philosophy. If you say *pratyakṣa* alone is a means of knowledge, in the sense, anything sensorily perceived alone is true and everything else is untrue, you create a philosophy. In fact, it is the philosophy of a *cārvāka*, a mechanical materialist. A person named Bṛhaspati was the expounder of this philosophy.

Perception is of two kinds. It can take place with or without the help of sense organs. Perception with the help of sense organs is qualified as *indriya-pratyakṣa,* direct sensory perception. Perception that takes place without the help of sense organs is called *sākṣi-pratyakṣa,* witness perception. In this perception, you—the witness, the knower—directly perceive. For instance, your hunger, your thirst, your emotions, the flow of time, the spatial situations—all these are known through witness perception. Here too, the result is direct knowledge. What is sensorily perceived needs sense organs; mere *sākṣin* cannot perceive, though *sākṣin* is very much there even in sensory perceptions. *Sākṣin* will always be present, but the sense organs are necessary additions in *indriya-pratyakṣa*. While sense organs negate each other, the *sākṣin* is always there in every perception. In the absence of all the sense organs also, the *sākṣin* continues to be there.

Our day-to-day life is conducted by a few more valid *pramāṇa*s, and they are very important. The first among them is *anumāna,* inference. It is a means of knowledge by which something is inferred through reasoning. In perception, reason is not employed. For instance, when you hear a dog barking, there is no reasoning employed in the perception of the particular sound. From the type of sound heard, one infers that there is a dog around even though it is not directly seen. The perception gives you certain datum or data, based upon which you use your reason and come to know something else.

You see *dhūma*, smoke, on the *parvata*, mountain. Both smoke and the mountain are directly seen to say *parvataḥ dhūmavān*—the mountain has smoke. This is direct perception. But instead of saying the mountain has smoke, we conclude that the mountain has fire—*parvataḥ vahnimān*. We do not see any fire at all; what we see is only a cloud of smoke, but our knowledge is *parvataḥ vahnimān*. There is certain reasoning, certain inner process of thinking involving certain steps between the perception that the mountain has smoke and the conclusion that the mountain has fire. This is *anumāna,* inference.

In the stock example 'the mountain has fire' what is the step between the perception of smoke and the conclusion that there is fire? You do not conclude that the mountain has a lot of elephants because you see smoke there! It is illogical. Now you can understand what is logic. What is illogical is not outside logic; it is within logic. Only then can you say it is illogical. When you say that there must be fire because you see smoke, there must be a connection between the smoke and fire which reveals an invariable co-presence, an invariable concomitance. Suppose, there is smoke without fire, sometimes, you cannot then arrive at a definite conclusion on seeing smoke. You will merely be doing some guesswork.

The smoke cannot be there without fire. Whenever there is smoke there must be fire. This is called *vyāpti,* invariable concomitance. You have to make sure whether the perception is of a cloud of smoke that keeps coming. If it is just a cloud of smoke, fire might have been there and gone, but the smoke is still there. If the smoke keeps coming, that means there must be fire. Fire can be present without producing smoke, but smoke cannot be present without the presence of fire. The invariable connection between smoke and fire is known from your daily perception in the kitchen and this is cited as example, *dṛṣṭānta*. An example holds the *vyāpti*. If you can show an instance where that invariable nature is contradicted, then your whole *anumāna* gets falsified. This is how reasoning is used in logic to gain ascertained knowledge, in our daily life as well as in scientific research. This way *anumāna* is accepted as a valid means of knowledge. If this is not accepted, then you may walk into the burning forest because you do not see fire, but only smoke.

This *anumāna* itself, when extended, is called *arthāpatti*, presumption. In this inference there is more than one step involved. Taking the stock example, I observe that Devadatta does not eat during the day. I part with him in the night. Again, I do not see him eating the next day. However, he does not lose weight. There are two situations here. Devadatta is not eating during the day and at the same time he does not lose weight. We have clear knowledge that one will lose weight if one does not eat. But Devadatta does not eat during the day and at the same time he does not lose weight. Since it is not possible for the two conditions to coexist, *anyathā anupapattau*, we make a logical conclusion that Devadatta eats during the night. Otherwise, it is not possible to maintain the same weight. This *arthāpatti*, presumption, is distinct from inference. What is arrived at by presumption cannot be arrived at by inference. Hence *arthāpatti* has to be counted separately as a means of knowledge.

What is inferentially known, what is presumptuously known is indirect knowledge. Indirect knowledge is as important as direct knowledge. A plane takes off and lands only by indirect knowledge. In accomplishing anything desirable or avoiding and getting rid of something undesirable, we require indirect knowledge.

We get indirect knowledge by yet another means. I have been told bison is an animal that is like a water buffalo. This knowledge helps me identify a bison that is similar to a water buffalo. Thus the indirect knowledge of similarity called *upamāna* leads me to direct knowledge of the bison.

We have another means of knowledge known as *anupalabdhi*. It is a very peculiar means of knowledge. All the means of knowledge we have seen above are meant to know a thing that exists. *Anupalabdhi* is a means of knowledge to know a thing that does not exist. Again, the stock example is *kara-tale ghaṭaḥ nāsti*, there is no pot on my hand. The absence of pot is not known by perception. Eyes only see objects in terms of the light reflected by them. So it is the hand alone that the eyes can see. The sense organs objectify only things that exist; the absence of a thing is not picked up by the sense organs. But you do come to know the absence of a thing. The means by which we know the absence is called *anupalabdhi*. We must know what exists as well as what does not.

We have one more means of knowledge. How do you know the existence of heaven? It is not by perception or inference or presumption—all these means of knowledge have no scope there. *Anupalabdhi* has no scope here, as we are talking of an existent heaven. Where there is access for the other three means of knowledge, there you have scope for *anupalabdhi*. A pot is perceived, and hence to know the absence of a second pot there, *anupalabdhi* is employed. A particular disease is inferred because there is absence of the symptoms of other diseases.

With reference to heaven you cannot say that there is heaven, nor can you say there is no heaven. How can we talk about heaven then? The whole humanity is holding on to the concept of heaven. The expression 'heaven' has entered our common usage also. We say, "For heaven's sake, do not do this." The only means of knowledge by which we come to know of heaven is the Veda. Hence, we call the Veda a separate means of knowledge.

Svarga, heaven, is a desirable place where the soul reaches after death with an appropriate body. There are many means for going to heaven. You have to perform the stipulated rituals and charities to gather *puṇya*, invisible good results, that take you there.

Also to know the existence of the *devatās*, deities, like Indra, Varuṇa, Agni and so on, the means of knowledge is only the Veda which is in the form of *śabda*, word. *Śabda* becomes a *pramāṇa* only when you have *śraddhā* in it. Lord Kṛṣṇa says in the *Bhagavad Gītā*,[1]—a person with *śraddhā* alone gains any knowledge.

The status given to the Veda as an independent means of knowledge cannot be questioned by one's perception, inference and so on, because the Veda is talking about a subject matter to which perception etc., have no access. So it is not contentious; like what I see is not contended by what I hear. Hearing and seeing are independent means of knowledge and, therefore, one does not contradict the other. Similarly, the Veda is an independent means of knowledge that cannot be questioned by any other means.

The Veda gives rise to certain knowledge that is useful. That is the difference between the Veda and the other means of knowledge. Perception can bring in for you knowledge that you may not use at all. As you walk in the outskirts of the city, you see rocks and pebbles that you do not care about. Perception will bring in all kinds of data, some of which you have no value for. In the Veda, however, there cannot be any useless material because the words are deliberately

---

[1] *śraddhāvān labhate jñānam*…(4.39)

used, and the messages are useful to someone or the other. For instance, a newspaper may have columns that contain information which is not useful to you, but useful to others. The 'wanted' column in the newspaper may not be read by a *sannyāsin*, but that does not mean the wanted column has no utility. Whatever is said in the Veda is useful. Thus, we have a subject matter that is useful to a human being but not available for other means of knowledge. That subject matter is available for knowing either directly or indirectly, depending upon the nature of it.

All the above *pramāṇas*, including the Veda, imply the presence of the *pramātṛ*, the knower. The knower operates these various means of knowledge. The Veda, as an independent *pramāṇa*, also presents Brahman as the cause of the world and equates Brahman to the *pramātṛ*, the knower. When the Veda talks about you as the cause of the world, that 'you' indicates purely the *pramātṛ*. This reveals an equation.

An equation is a necessity when there is a fact and the fact is not known, is hidden in the apparent difference. The apparent difference is very clear. The *jīva* is an individual confined to this body-mind-sense-complex, limited in knowledge, power and so on. Brahman, whom I come to know only through the Veda, the *śāstra*, is just the opposite. The difference is obvious. When Brahman is equated to me, there is a hidden oneness in the vision of the *śāstra*.

The revelation of the oneness by the *śāstra* implies the disappearance of the *pramātṛ*. The *pramātṛ* has a certain limitation, and while retaining that limitation the *pramātṛ* is not going to discover, "I am Brahman." Therefore, the *pramātṛtva*, the status of being a knower, on the part of the *jīva* is to be negated, and it is negatable.

Negation has no meaning if it is not negatable. If *pramātṛtva* is negatable, then it is not an intrinsic property of the *ātman*. If it is not a property of the *atman*, it need not be negated. For example, you need not negate the potness from the flower because flower has no potness. So, the negation itself tells us that *pramātṛtva* is considered a property of the *ātman*. Otherwise, there is no necessity for negation. Since it can be negated, *pramātṛtva* is not an intrinsic property of the *ātman*. If it is not an intrinsic property, from the standpoint of the essential nature of the *atman*, there is no *pramātṛtva*. Thus, the negation itself reveals that what is negated is only an incidental property. An incidental property is assumed to be the property of the *ātman*, and that assumption is what is negated. If an incidental property is known as an incidental property, then there is no problem; we do not require negating it. But if the incidental property is taken to be the intrinsic property of the *ātman*, then the assumption—that the property belongs to the *ātman*—is to be negated. The assumption is purely a superimposition and hence negatable. Being negatable it is negated.

Again, the *śāstra* presents Brahman as *satyaṁ jñānam anantam*, existence-knowledge-limitlessness. So, nothing is separate from that Brahman. Brahman is non-dual. Non-duality necessarily implies oneness, and therefore, the *jīva* cannot be separate from it. *Jīva* plus Brahman is not possible. The truth of the *jīva* is bound to be *satyaṁ jñānam anantam*. Therefore, the *jīva* and Īśvara are essentially one truth. The *īśvaratva* as well as *jīvatva* are not the intrinsic properties of Īśvara and *jīva*. In essence there is no difference. That means the difference becomes what we call *mithyā*. The teaching "You are Brahman," therefore, stays. By this, the *pramātṛ* himself is negated by the *śāstra*. To reveal this truth, one does not have any other means of knowledge, save the Veda.

With reference to heaven, etc., one has no means of knowing, and therefore it becomes the subject matter of the Veda. However, in understanding about this heaven, etc., the *pramātṛ* is necessary and the *pramātṛ* has to exist in order to know that there is heaven, that there is rebirth, there is *puṇya*, *pāpa* and so on. It is the Vedic knowledge acquired by the *pramātṛ*. Even though the Veda operates independently as a *pramāṇa*, there is a necessity for the *pramātṛ* with reference to the first portion of the Veda dealing with various limited means and ends.

In the last portion known as Vedanta, the Veda talks about the 'I'. I am someone who is already existent.

I do not require any means of knowledge to know that 'I am'. Neither do I have to employ *pratyakṣa* to know my existence, nor *anumāna* and so on, to know that I am existent. I am there; therefore all these means of knowledge operate. I am there; therefore the Veda also operates.

How then, *ātman* is the subject matter of Vedanta? What Vedanta has to tell about me is to be known by me without retaining the *pramātṛ*. In the operation of every other means of knowledge I remain as the *pramātṛ*, knower. I will never be able to know myself, operating the means of knowledge I have, giving up the *pramātṛ* in me. Since the notion 'I am a *pramātṛ*' has to be negated, the truth of the *pramātṛ* becomes the subject matter of the Vedanta. The *pramātṛ* is swallowed in the process of knowing. The *pramātṛ* does not continue to exist to know, "Oh! This is Brahman." Brahman is not going to be objectified, either directly or indirectly, by the *pramātṛ*. Everything else is directly or indirectly objectified. There is no way of this *pramātṛ* stumbling upon Brahman because *pramātṛ* is Brahman. One, thus, requires another *pramāṇa* and that *pramāṇa* is *śabda*. Therefore, *ātma-jñāna*, self-knowledge, also is included in the Veda.

If you analyse the scriptures of the various religions in the world, you find that their subject matter is entirely different. The *pramātṛ* has to know about a heaven; one should look upon oneself as one to be saved, and accept a prophet or a saviour, and then hope with sheer faith that one will go to heaven. The Veda also, in its first portion, talks about heaven and its means but as a time-bound field of experience. The scriptural teaching ends there. Vedanta begins where they end.

This subject matter, self-knowledge itself, is *upaniṣad*. It qualifies to be the subject matter of the Veda because it is *anadhigata,* not known by other five means of knowledge and cannot be known. The words of the *upaniṣad* have *phalavat arthabodhakatvam,* the capacity to reveal the subject matter that is fruitful.

Revealing a subject matter which is useful and which is not known by other means of knowledge is the criterion for being an independent *pramāṇa*. We can apply this criterion for the first portion of the Veda. Heaven is a subject matter of the first portion of the Veda. It is *phalavat,* useful, for the one who wants to go there. It is not known by other means of knowledge. So too, subject matters like the *agnihotra* ritual, *puṇya-pāpa* and so on. Knowing what is *pāpa,* you avoid acts of *pāpa,* the cause for *duḥkha,* sorrow. Knowing what is *puṇya,* you perform acts of *puṇya* so that you can gain *sukha,* pleasure. So, both *puṇya* and *pāpa* are fruitful, and at the same time, not known to us by any other means.

If the Veda says something that is already known to me, then that is purely an *anuvāda,* re-statement.

For instance, it is said *ghṛtena juhuyāt*, may one perform this ritual by an oblation of clarified butter offered unto the fire for the given *devatā*. Here, I know clarified butter. The Veda does not reveal clarified butter. It does the *anuvāda* of clarified butter. What it reveals is that clarified butter is the oblation in a particular ritual and that is not known to me. Therefore it is *pramāṇa-vākya*, revealing sentence. When the Veda makes a reference to bricks, it is not *pramāṇa*, but it is a *pramāṇa* for the number of bricks necessary for creating an altar. That is why, even if there is a statement in the Veda that seems to contradict what we can figure out with our means of knowledge, the Veda is not contradicted. It is because the Veda is not a *pramāṇa* for that subject matter. Therefore, no other means of knowledge can contradict the Veda.

The Veda is not scientific. Without giving much thought to what a *pramāṇa* is, people say that the Veda is scientific. Maybe that is purely *anuvāda*. But it is dangerous to say that the Veda is scientific, because if the Veda is science, then modern science is definitely better than the Veda, which has only words without any supporting evidence. The Veda then becomes an obsolete science. It can only be admired as a record of how, in those days, they knew many things without the aid of modern labs. That they knew something of this sort does not really make any sense to me in terms of the Veda being a *pramāṇa*. They knew something, but definitely we know something more and something more advanced. That is not what a *pramāṇa* is.

What is *anadhigata,* a subject matter to which I have no access, alone is the subject matter of the Veda. It is *svataḥ pramāṇam,* a valid means by itself. You can contradict what it says only when it says something which is available within the means of knowledge you have. To contradict it, the fact of the subject in question is known differently. Then the *viṣaya,* subject matter is not beyond the scope of the means of knowledge you have. If this is the position of the Veda as a means of knowledge, how anyone can contradict it? It stands untouched by any other means of knowledge.

The Veda cannot be dismissed, though one can be indifferent to what it says. That indifference is applicable to all means of knowledge. For instance, in perception, the eyes bring a lot of information, and you can be indifferent to most of it. Similarly, the Veda reveals a lot of things. For instance, it says that you may perform a ritual called *putra-kāmeṣṭi* if you are desirous of progeny. This is not going to interest a person who has no desire for more children. Naturally, he can only be indifferent to the ritual.

In the end portion, the Veda talks about *ātman,* I. It reveals that I am Brahman. This fact is also *anadhigata,* not known by any other means of knowledge because it is the very nature of the *pramātṛ.*

It is *phalavat;* it is desirable. Even though one has to choose to have self-knowledge, it is not open to choice. Really speaking, there is no choice in *ātma-jñāna,* in the sense that, when a person has gone through a life of relating to Īśvara properly and has a matured mind with certain *viveka,* there is no choice. There is no choice whether[2] I should gain *mokṣa.*

When you choose *mokṣa,* you have already found that you have nothing to choose any more. That maturity is what life has to teach a person. *Mokṣa* is a matured choice, meaning you have no other choice.

If I come to appreciate that I have no choice in gaining the knowledge of *ātman,* then I have no choice in employing an appropriate *pramāṇa* having *anadhigatatva* and *phalavatva. Anadhigatatva* is there because *ātman* being Brahman, the cause of the world, cannot be known by other means. *Phalavatva* is there because it gives freedom from the becoming life, *saṁsāra.*

The Veda is a *pramāṇa* for *karma-jñāna* and *ātma-jñāna.* When it talks about heaven and so on, one has to simply accept what it says. That is why *mīmāṁsā,* analysis of words, becomes important. The Veda being a *śabda-pramāṇa,* one should not bring one's own

---

[2] Whether or not is a common expression but the correct usage is only 'whether' without being followed by 'or not'. Whether one likes this, grammatically this is right (Author).

subjectivity, one's own conclusions into the Veda. One has to understand what the Veda says as it is. One must be highly dispassionate to gain that understanding. One must have *śraddhā*, respect, for those words. Only then can one understand what it has to say. Otherwise, one can twist its meaning to one's own liking. To avoid this kind of twisting, we have a highly evolved system of analysis of words. In the process we come to analyse and correct our habitual ways of wrong thinking.

In this sophisticated method of analysis we take into account what was said before and what is said later. If the earlier and later statements have to be meaningful, there should be no contradiction. In ascertaining the meaning of the words, grammar, semantics and linguistics are used. Human experiences are also pressed into service to understand what does a Vedic sentence mean.

The Veda should not contradict itself. It should not contradict human experience. Nor should it contradict any knowledge you gain through the other valid means of knowledge, like perception and so on. The analysis determining the meaning that does not contradict is called *mīmāṁsā*.

Coming back to the difference between the two sections of the Veda, the knowledge given by the *karma-kāṇḍa* is certainly going to be indirect. The words talking about heaven give rise to knowledge that is bound to be *parokṣa,* indirect. The knowledge that the performance of a given ritual will give me *puṇya* that will take me to heaven is purely *parokṣa.* Though it is only *śraddhā,* we call it *parokṣa,* born of Veda to which we have given the status of a means of knowledge. I have *śraddhā* in it. There is no other basis to accept it, muchless there is one to dismiss it; I just take it as it is. I may not be interested in heaven—that is a different matter.

When words—whether they are from a given person or from an enlightened person or from the Veda itself—talk about an object that is away from you, the knowledge gathered would be *parokṣa.* If the object is just you, which is already self-evident, the knowledge will be *aparokṣa,* immediate. Here, the subject matter is 'you' as the very nature of the sought, which is why you should be interested in it. Brahman is said to be the subject matter because you happen to be Brahman and you are the subject matter. So the knowledge here is immediate unlike the knowledge of the *karma-kāṇḍa.*

This *aparokṣa-jñāna* given by Vedanta gives you a result that resolves the result-hunting seeker. You have no choice in employing it. You have to study it. Vedanta is also called *upaniṣad.* The word '*upaniṣad*' means *ātma-jñāna* that is *phalavat.*

Upaniṣad is a descriptive word with two *upasargas,* prefixes. One is *upa,* the other is *ni;* the word is *sad.*

In fact, *sad* is a *dhātu*, root, which is not used as a *pada*, word. It requires either a nominal or verbal suffix to become a word. For certain words this suffix comes and goes away after converting the *dhātu* into a word. Here, the suffix '*kvip*' which is not visible, converts the root *sad* into a word imparting the meaning of agent of action indicated by the root meaning. This root reveals the action of *viśaraṇa*, wearing out, *gamana*, reaching, knowing and *avasādana*, putting an end to.

What is it that does these actions? That is indicated by the two prefixes *upa-ni*. The prefix *upa* means something near. Brahman is never separate from you, it is you, yet, it is looked upon as something to be gained, to be known. If Brahman is me, what separates me from Brahman is ignorance. Ignorance about myself being Brahman makes me a seeker of Brahman. The prefix *upa*, therefore, means Brahman, the very one sought after in life.

The prefix *ni* means *niścaya-jñāna*, clear knowledge, the knowledge that Brahman is indeed myself. Is the word 'knowledge' not enough? Where is the need for the adjective *niścaya*, 'clear' here? In order to understand the revelations such as '*tat tvam asi*, you are that', you have to get *vākyārtha*, the meaning of the sentence. *Padārtha*, the meaning of words, will not work. To see the meaning of that equation 'you are that' you require to resolve many doubts through *vicāra*, inquiry.

The whole *pramāṇa* pursuit is *vicārātmaka,* in the form of an inquiry and analysis. Therefore, you have got to ascertain what you know is correct. There, the prefix *ni* is appropriately used.

You have to know for good what is meant by the prefix *upa,* something that is close to you, that is sought after by you, that is yourself. That means there is ignorance, and therefore, knowledge is necessary. Because it is the truth of the knower, me, it is not the subject matter of other means of knowledge. It is *phalavat* because it wears out and also puts an end to all undesirable things. Mere wearing out is not enough. The host of *anartha*s may revive and come back after some time. Hence, the other meaning of the root, *avasādana,* putting an end to, is also relevant. There is a positive gain too in this result. The knowledge makes you discover 'I am Brahman' positively. So, the criteria *phalavat-artha-bodhakatva* and *anadhigatatva* are said in that one word *upaniṣad. Upanisad* will become *upaniṣad* due to a grammar rule that prescribes the change of the letter '*s*' following '*i*' into '*ṣ*'.

The word, '*upaniṣad*' means both the self-knowledge as well as the text in the form of words that reveals this knowledge. The knowledge is *upaniṣad,* and the book that conveys that knowledge is also called *upaniṣad*. This *upaniṣad* is otherwise called Vedanta.

Vedanta means that which is at the end of the Veda. It is not end of knowledge; it is purely a positional name. There is a discussion on the position itself in the *Brahma Sūtra*. The subject matter of any *upaniṣad* is the same self-knowledge, whether it is *Īśāvāsyopaniṣad, Kenopaniṣad, Kaṭhopaniṣad, Praśnopaniṣad, Muṇḍakopaniṣad, Māṇḍūkyopaniṣad, Taittirīyopaniṣad, Aitareyopaniṣad, Chāndogyopaniṣad* or *Bṛhadāraṇyakopaniṣad*.

If the subject matter is the same, why are there so many *upaniṣad*s? They are all from the four Vedas. Suppose you are studying your branch of the Veda, it must have minimum one *upaniṣad* so that the Vedic vision of you as Brahman is available for you. So, we have *upaniṣad*s in all the four Vedas and the ten mentioned above, form the texts commented upon by *Ācārya* Śaṅkara.

Each *upaniṣad* implies a teacher-student dialogue. Each teacher has his own way of looking at the whole thing; the Veda thus presents this subject matter from different standpoints through different *upaniṣad*s. Certain topics may be emphasised in one *upaniṣad* while some other topics may be highlighted in others. Therefore, you see a few *upaniṣad*s from different standpoints so that you understand the subject matter properly.

From the commentary of Śaṅkara we learn that there were other commentaries in the teaching tradition prevalent during his time[3] and he talks about them. Even though the *upaniṣads* have already been analysed, he says, "I am going to do this commentary because there are different contentions." He tells what is wrong with some of them. He himself talks about *sampradāya*, the method of teaching. Śaṅkara had captured and presented in his commentaries the whole vision, including the tradition of teaching itself. He not only shows how a *mantra* should be understood, but also analyses all other possible problems that existed before him, and the contemporary notions that were floating around in his time. A modern teacher should have the same spirit and deal with all the contemporary notions. They need to be considered and negated where they go wrong.

To distinguish one *upaniṣad* from another, an adjective is prefixed to the word *upaniṣad*. *Praśnopaniṣad*, for example, contains six questions, *praśnas*, and that makes its name. *Īśāvāsyopaniṣad* is so named because it begins with the words *īśa vāsyam*. Similarly, *Kenopaniṣad*[4] takes its name from the first

---

[3] तदिदं गीताशास्त्रं समस्तवेदार्थसारसंग्रहभूतं दुर्विज्ञेयार्थम् । तदर्थाविष्करणायानेकैः विवृत-पदपदार्थ-वाक्यार्थ-न्यायमप्यत्यन्त-विरुद्धानेकार्थत्वेन लौकिकैर्गृह्यमाणमुपलभ्याहं विवेकतः अर्थ-निर्धारणार्थं संक्षेपतो विवरणं करिष्यमि । (श्रीमद्भगवद्गीता उपोद्घात-भाष्यम्)

[4] Due to grammatical rules governing the combination of Sanskrit letters, *kena + upaniṣad* becomes *Kenopaniṣad*.

word of the text, *kena*, meaning by what or by whom. There is no other meaning whatsoever.

Śaṅkara wrote two types of commentary on *Kenopaniṣad*, enhancing its importance for those who seek self-knowledge. One is the *pada-bhāṣya*, a commentary based upon the words of the *mantra*s, and the other is *vākya-bhāṣya*, a commentary based upon the theme.

PRAYER

शान्तिपाठः

ॐ आप्यायन्तु ममाङ्गानि वाक्प्राणश्चक्षुः श्रोत्रमथो बलमिन्द्रियाणि च सर्वाणि । सर्वं ब्रह्मौपनिषदम् । माहं ब्रह्म निराकुर्याम् । मा मा ब्रह्म निराकरोत् । अनिराकरणमस्त्वनिराकरणं मेऽस्तु । तदात्मनि निरते य उपनिषत्सु धर्मास्ते मयि सन्तु । ते मयि सन्तु ॥
ॐ शान्तिः शान्तिः शान्तिः ॥

om āpyāyantu mamāṅgāni vākprāṇaścakṣuḥ śrotram atho balamindriyāṇi ca sarvāṇi, sarvaṁ brahmaupaniṣadam, māhaṁ brahma nirākuryām, mā mā brahma nirākarot, anirākaraṇamastvanirākaraṇaṁ me'stu, tadātmani nirate ya upaniṣatsu dharmāste mayi santu, te mayi santu. om śāntiḥ śāntiḥ śāntiḥ.

om – om; *āpyāyantu* – may grow in strength; *mama* – my; *aṅgāni* – limbs; *vāk* – organ of speech; *prāṇaḥ* – physiological system; *cakṣuḥ* – eye; *śrotram* – ear; *atha* – also; *u* – definitely; *balam* – capacity; *indriyāṇi* – sense organs; *ca* – and; *sarvāṇi* – all; *sarvam* – everything; *brahma* – (is) Brahman; *aupaniṣadam* – revealed by the *upaniṣad*; *mā* – not; *aham* – I; *brahma* – Brahman; *nirākuryām* – reject; *mā* – not; *mā* – me; *brahma* –

Brahman; *nirākarot* – reject; *anirākaraṇam* – non-rejection; *astu* – let it be; *anirākaraṇam*– non-rejection; *me* – for me; *astu* – let it be; *tad*– that; *ātmani* – in the self; *nirate* – who is committed to; *ye* – which; *upaniṣatsu* – in the *upaniṣads*; *dharmāḥ* – values and attitudes; *te*– they; *mayi* – in me; *santu* – let them be; *te*– they; *mayi* – in me; *santu* – let them be; *om*– om; *śāntiḥ* – peace; *śāntiḥ* – peace; *śāntiḥ*– peace

May my limbs such as speech, eyes and ears, the capacity (strength), and all other organs—grow (be efficient). Everything is Brahman that is known through the *upaniṣads*. May I not reject Brahman. May Brahman not reject me. Let there be no rejection (of me) by Brahman. Let there be no rejection of Brahman on my part. Let all the values and attitudes mentioned in the *upaniṣads* be in me who is committed to the pursuit of knowledge of Brahman. Let them abide in me. Om. Peace. Peace. Peace.

This is the prayer verse for *Kenopaniṣad*. Every *upaniṣad* begins with a prayer. Generally, the prayer of the *upaniṣads* belonging to a given Veda is the same. The *Kenopaniṣad* is from the *Sāmaveda* and all the *upaniṣads* that belong to *Sāmaveda* will have this prayer. Similarly, the prayer for all the *upaniṣads* belonging to the *Kṛṣṇa Yajurveda* is the famous *saha nāvavatu...*, even though the *Taittirīyopaniṣad* has one more prayer chant in *śanno mitraśśaṁ varuṇaḥ...* For the *Śukla Yajurveda, pūrṇam adaḥ pūrṇam idam...* is the prayer verse. *Īśāvāsyopaniṣad* and *Bṛhadāraṇyakopaniṣad*, which belong to the *Śukla Yajurveda*, start with *pūrṇam adaḥ pūrṇam idam*. For the *Ṛgveda, vāṅ me manasi pratiṣṭhitā, mano me vāci pratiṣṭhitam...* is the prayer verse. *Aitareyopaniṣad* is from the *Ṛgveda*. There are many *upaniṣads* in the *Atharvaveda*, like *Muṇḍaka, Māṇḍūkya*, and so on, which have the prayer verse starting with *bhadraṁ karṇebhiḥ śṛṇuyāma devāḥ*.... At the beginning of a class the relevant prayer verse is chanted both by the teacher and the student. Here the *Kenopaniṣad* begins with the prayer—*āpyāyantu mamāṅgāni...*

Āpyāyantu mama aṅgāni: Let my limbs grow and gain strength. Let them be able to do things that have to be done by them. What are those *aṅgas*, limbs? *Vāk*, organ of speech, *prāṇaḥ*, the physiological system, *cakṣuḥ*, eyes, and so on. *Prāṇaḥ* refers to the health of the entire system. Let my *samāna*, digestion, be good. Let my *apāna*, functions of evacuation, take place properly. Let all my *indriyas–karmendriyas* and *jñānendriyas*–be healthy.

This is a prayer in the section of *jñāna*, knowledge. The subject matter decides the nature of the prayer. When I go to a teacher to learn Brahman, I pray, "May my sense organs all grow well and be healthy;"

the health I seek is only for *mokṣa*.[5] When there is health, I can pursue knowledge. I can sit and listen to the scriptures. The health has to be conducive because the physical body is considered to be the primary means for acquiring *dharma*, that is, doing *karma* as well as for gaining *mokṣa*.

A question may arise here as to whether the *jīva* is qualified or the body is qualified. The *jīva* is qualified; every worm is a *jīva* but a worm's body is not qualified. This *jīva*, assuming a human body, or one equivalent to a human body, has the faculty of choice. Once the choice is there, then the *puruṣārtha*s come to the fore. Then *dharma* becomes a *puruṣārtha* and *mokṣa* becomes the *puruṣārtha*. The *jīva* in the human body is the one who is an *adhikārin*, one who is qualified, and therefore, the *adhikāri-śarīra* is the means for *dharma* / *karma* and *mokṣa* . That is why it is said elsewhere that it is rare to get a human body—*jantūnāṁ nara-janma durlabham*.[6] If *mokṣa* is not accomplished in this human body, then this human body is a nuisance, because it gives rise to all our complexes. In this body alone one accumulates more and more *puṇya* and *pāpa*, thereby perpetuating the *saṁsāra*. At least if *mokṣa* is attempted in this *janma*, that is a step forward. It will carry over to next *janma*.

---

[5] ब्रह्मप्राप्त्यनुकूलतया बलं वृद्धिं प्राप्नुवन्तु - may they grow healthily, may they become mature so that they are conducive in my gaining the knowledge of Brahman.

[6] *Vivekacūḍāmaṇi* verse 1

One can only make an attempt; everything else is automatically taken care of.

This prayer has two aspects. It is a prayer for the growth, *vṛddhi,* and health of all the organs. It is also a prayer that the activities of all the organs be mature enough to help me gain knowledge of Brahman. Let them not be active in a manner that is not conducive for gaining the knowledge of Brahman.

The sense organs themselves do not disturb; the disturbance comes in the form of the mind's fancy for a particular enjoyment caused by one's sense appetites. Even though gaining Brahman is not accomplished through perception or action, still, all these organs are necessary; ears, for instance, to listen to the *śāstra,* and so on. The word *atha* stands for all other organs not mentioned here and '*u*' means indeed.

Sarvaṁ brahma aupaniṣadam: Everything that is here is Brahman, and this Brahman is revealed through the *upaniṣad*. *Aupaniṣadam* means that which is known only through the words of the *upaniṣad*. *Aupaniṣadaṁ brahma* is a very important phrase, often quoted. Brahman which is revealed by the words of the *upaniṣad* as the cause of the *jagat,* as yourself, is *sarva,* everything.

The word *sarva,* all, here is not in the relative sense of predominance. When you say, "All the people are rich in this city," it does not mean that all of them are rich. It is an expression indicating that there are a lot of rich people. It comes under *chatri-nyāya,* an analogy of umbrella-holders. A *nyāya* is an analogy by which you arrive at a general conclusion. When the majority of people carry umbrella in a gathering, you say, "they all carry umbrellas," even though there may be persons without umbrella. Whereas, *sarva* here means, all without exception. *Vidita*, anything known, and *avidita*, anything unknown, is the meaning of the word 'all'. Brahman that is revealed by the *upaniṣad*s is everything.

In the *Mahābhārata* there is a beautiful episode to illustrate this fact. When Bhīma went in search of an exotic flower *saugandhika*, in the Himalayas, he came across an old monkey lying on the way. Upon Bhīma's order to move, clearing the way, the monkey said, "I am too old, I cannot move, you just jump over me and go." Bhīma said, "I cannot jump over you because *paramātman*, who is gained through knowledge, is pervading you. I cannot show disregard to *nirguṇaṁ brahma paramātmā* by jumping over you. If I were not taught, then I could do that. In fact, I can cross a mountain, just as Hanumān crossed the ocean." He did not know he was talking to Hanumān. Hanumān smiled, "That is good."

How does one know Brahman is everything? One comes to hear or read about Brahman being everything and the knowledge of Brahman is *mokṣa*. Therefore, one wants to know Brahman. Brahman being *aupaniṣadam*, one must necessarily study *upaniṣad* now.

Brahman that is everything becomes the worshipful Lord and the prayer is based upon this knowledge about Brahman being everything.

Further, *māhaṁ brahma nirākuryām*: May I not be indifferent to Brahman. *Ahaṁ brahma mā nirākuryām.* This is a very interesting expression. May I not reject Brahman. Rejection can happen only if I choose not to know. The choice is pointed out here. May I not dismiss the pursuit of Brahman by saying that there is no Brahman. May I choose to know Brahman.

There are different types of rejection possible. The *śāstra* tells you, "You are that (Brahman)–*tat-tvam-asi.*" The first thing that occurs in your mind is "how can I be that Brahman?" One cannot say that the *śāstra* says that I am not Brahman.

If one were to understand what exactly the *śāstra* has to say, that is called *śravaṇa*. The word *śravaṇa* itself means a dispassionate inquiry into the words of the *śāstra* to find out what is its *tātparya*, vision, what it wants to convey to me. This is the first stage of *śravaṇa* where *tātparya-niścaya* takes place.

The second stage of *śravaṇa* is just completely submitting oneself to the *pramāṇa* for the *pramāṇa* to do its job. Once the *tātparya-niścaya* is there, the mind relaxes and then what is unfolded by the *śāstra* becomes clear. If the *tātparya-niścaya* is not there, at least *śraddhā* must be there. If Brahman is limitless it cannot be separate from you; any other Brahman will become limited. Being not you, and like you, Brahman has to be one among the countless beings and things. Knowledge of Brahman that is not you is as good as the knowledge of any one thing in the world—it cannot liberate you. *Caitanya,* consciousness is Brahman and that *caitanya* is just you.

If Brahman is oneself, then what about the *jagat*? The *jagat* being non-separate from *caitanya,* is also oneself. Thus, one gets to know all that is oneself. One has to understand Brahman in that form, as *sarva.* "I am God" is a statement that has to be understood properly. The one who says, "I am God," is aware of what he or she is saying and the listener also should be able to understand what the person says. Even if the listener does not understand, the one who says, "I am God" definitely should mean it.

However, in the beginning one has to see the possibility of this vision; only then will one not reject Brahman. To reject Brahman is to reject oneself. But people do reject. It shows that one does not have adequate grace in one's life. Maybe the Lord's grace was good enough for the person to study the Veda and have the language, etc., but not for anything more.

We cannot say that the *dvaita* philosophy was presented by its founders in keeping with the needs of the people of those days, that people did not require a philosophy that swallowed devotion, and that people needed devotion. This is not right. People need truth. Vedanta does not in any way affect one's devotion. In fact, Vedanta, if properly taught, only generates devotion and strengthens it. If one understands the *śāstra* properly, then one cannot change its vision just because one does not understand it. One can teach those topics of the *śāstra* that people require and understand, but for people's sake one cannot distort the *śāstra*. One who is already committed to a dualistic philosophy would reject the non-dual Brahman.

Mā mā brahma nirākarot: May Brahman also not reject me. Here *brahma* means Īśvara, Brahman as the cause of the *jagat*, as the source of all *karma-phala*. May he shower his grace upon me so that my pursuit of Brahman will be successful. I am a helpless, ordinary individual bound by the innumerable laws of the Lord, and naturally any small mishap may disturb my pursuit.

Until one gains this knowledge, let his grace not run out. The grace has to last. Otherwise, one does start all right, but stops somewhere halfway—like a car that starts, but stops at the wrong place with both the home and the gas station far apart. Many problems crop up, and thereby, one is not able to pursue the spiritual path successfully. So one makes a prayer: "May you be on my side always, may your grace not run out having given me a push."

May the *guru* who is in the form of Brahman, not reject me. The *guru* is teaching me '*tat tvam asi,* you are that'. If you are that Brahman, the *guru* is not going to be something else. Naturally, he is also that Brahman. So, let Brahman in the form of the *guru* be available for me and let him teach me; that is also meant in this prayer. We require both Īśvara's grace as well as *guru*'s grace.

Anirākaraṇam astu anirākaraṇaṁ me 'stu: Let there be no rejection from Īśvara and let there be no rejection of Īśvara on my part. What was said before is confirmed in these two lines. Let there be love for the pursuit of Brahman. Let Īśvara keep me in view. This is certainly a prayer asking for grace. Bhagavān is also a fountain of grace; you have to tap it.

Again, may I have the right attitude, so that I will not give up my pursuit saying, "I have tried—I do not any more care for this Brahman knowledge." One should pursue Vedanta until one understands, "I am Brahman;" that is called trying. In fact, there is no trying, really speaking, to be Brahman; you are already Brahman. You have to keep pursuing until you understand that fact.

A *pramāṇa* always functions that way. One cannot say, "I have tried to see colours with my eyes; I have failed. Therefore I am going to try some other means." One has to correct one's eyes to see. Just because one cannot see with one's eyes, one cannot use one's nose to see. So, one prays, "Let there be no rejection of Brahman on my part." So, a prayer is made to cover everything else that is necessary to gain this knowledge.

Tadātmani nirate ye upaniṣatsu dharmāḥ, te mayi santu, te mayi santu: May all the values and attitudes that are mentioned in the *upaniṣads* abide in me who is pursuing this self-knowledge. *Ye upaniṣatsu dharmāḥ*-those virtues mentioned in the *upaniṣads*. *Dharma* means all values and attitudes such as *śama*, mastery over the ways of thinking; *dama*, discipline over the sense pursuits; *uparati*, renunciation; *titikṣā*, a capacity to face all difficulties with a healthy attitude; *śraddhā*, faith in the words of the *śāstra*, and *samādhāna*, absorption, that are mentioned in the *upaniṣads*[7] as necessary for the one in pursuit of this knowledge. *Te mayi santu*, let them be in me. What kind of me? *Tadātmani nirate mayi*, me who is desirous of the knowledge of Brahman that is *ātman*. *Tad* means *brahma* that is known through *upaniṣad*. *Nirate* means in the one who revels, who loves the knowledge of *ātman* being Brahman, who is a *jijñāsu*. Let all the required qualifications be with me so that the *aupaniṣadaṁ brahma* will become clear to me.

---

[7] तस्मादेवंविच्छान्तो दान्त उपरतस्तितिक्षुः समाहितो भूत्वा आत्मन्येवात्मानं पश्यति । (बृहदारण्यक-काण्व-शाखा 4.4.23), तस्मादेवंविच्छान्तो दान्त उपरतस्तितिक्षुः श्रद्धावित्तो भूत्वा आत्मन्येवात्मानं पश्येत् (बृहदारण्यक-माध्यन्दिन-शाखा 4.2.28).

The qualifications in me are now in small measure. They have brought about an inclination in me to study the *upaniṣad*. Let them be in abundance, in the measure that is necessary for me to gain the fruits of the study. Let me become an *adhikārin*, a student qualified to understand the vision of the *upaniṣad*.

Here, the qualifications prayed for include both the *bahiraṅga-sādhana*s, external means, and *antaraṅga-sādhana*s, inner means. All the daily rituals and duties are external means. They help us gain *antaḥkaraṇa-śuddhi*. The inner means are *śama*, *śraddhā*, and so on, which help us to focus ourselves in the pursuit, and *śravaṇa-manana-nididhyāsana* are the direct means for knowledge. "Let me follow all of them so that I can gain this end," is the prayer. The repetition of *te mayi santu* is for emphasis.

Om śāntiḥ śāntiḥ śāntiḥ: Let there be freedom from all obstacles. *Śānti* is invoked three times here for warding off *tāpa-traya*, obstructions from three sources—*ādhidaivika*, *ādhibhautika* and *ādhyātmika*. The first one is obstacle over which I have no control, like earthquake and so on. The second one is from sources over which I have no immediate control, like people around who can cause problems. The third source is myself. These are obstructions centred on one's own body, senses and the mind. Let all of them be adequately blessed so that I can gain this knowledge.

CHAPTER 1

Mantra 1

ॐ केनेषितं पतति प्रेषितं मनः
केन प्राणः प्रथमः प्रैति युक्तः।
केनेषितां वाचमिमां वदन्ति
चक्षुः श्रोत्रं क उ देवो युनक्ति ॥ १.१ ॥

om keneṣitaṁ patati preṣitaṁ manaḥ
kena prāṇaḥ prathamaḥ praiti yuktaḥ,
keneṣitāṁ vācamimāṁ vadanti
cakṣuḥ śrotraṁ ka u devo yunakti (1.1)

om – om; *kena* – by what; *iṣitam* – willed; *patati* – lands upon; *preṣitam* – prompted; *manaḥ* – the mind; *kena* – by what; *prāṇaḥ* – the vital air; *prathamaḥ* – the foremost; *praiti* – goes in and out; *yuktaḥ* – united with; *kena* – by what; *iṣitām* – willed; *vācam* – words; *imām* – these; *vadanti* – speak; *cakṣuḥ* – eye; *śrotram* – ear; *kaḥ* – which; *u* – indeed; *devaḥ* – effulgent being; *yunakti* – unites

Willed by whom or prompted in whose presence does the mind land upon its objects? United with whom does the breath go in and out? Willed by whom do (people) speak these words? Which effulgent being unites the eyes and ears (with its functions)?

This *upaniṣad*, like all other *upaniṣads*, is in the form of a dialogue. The *upaniṣads* may or may not mention the names of the teacher and the student. In *Praśnopaniṣad* Pippalāda is the teacher and there are six students whose names are mentioned. Their questions and the teacher's answers constitute the *upaniṣad*.

In this *upaniṣad* the names are not mentioned, but the dialogue is presented, revealing the *sampradāya*, the method of acquiring this knowledge. It is something to be acquired with the help of a teacher and that is indicated through the dialogue. Again, this subject matter is to be gained without any doubt. A dialogue implies the resolution of doubt, for which a teacher-student dialogue is unavoidable.

Dialogues do not always resolve doubts in disciplines of knowledge that are growing. They often create more questions. But in Vedanta the doubts resolve, because the subject matter cannot be improved upon further. We are talking about the limitless, the partless. Either the partless is understood or not understood. The *śāstra* is very clear about the vision it wants to convey and this is the only vision that can be handed over to another person, totally. Nothing else is understood totally and therefore cannot be handed over totally. The *vastu* being the self-revealing you, all doubts can be resolved. So, a dialogue here is more than meaningful; it is fulfilling.

Further, what is to be negated to gain the vision is endless. The vision of one non-dual Brahman is pitted against one million notions. Every notion in the mind of the student has to be negated. The study implies the total removal of all wrong notions, doubts and vagueness, leading to total clarity. Whether the student raises questions, the *śāstra* itself asks questions and answers them. Therefore, a dialogue is inevitable in understanding Brahman. Thus, we have a dialogue here and it starts with a question, *kena*, by whom?

The nature of oneself is generally taken for granted. That is questioned here. The student asks about the nature of 'I,' but phrases the question in a very peculiar way.

Kena iṣitaṁ preṣitaṁ manaḥ patati: Prompted by whom, does the mind land upon a given object? The mind lands upon different objects; it begins to dwell upon different things. One does not even plan to think of a given object, but the mind suddenly seems to land upon the object. Does the mind itself move from object to object? Or is there someone[8] who is behind the mind making the mind think of something? Does that person exercise any will to make my mind think, or is that person a non-willing *vastu* in whose presence the mind behaves as it does?

---

[8] केन कर्त्रा इषितं इष्टम् अभिप्रेतं सद् मनः पतति गच्छति स्वविषयं प्रति । (केनभाष्यम्)
Desired by whom the mind goes towards its objects?

The verb *iṣitam* should be read as *eṣitam.*[9] The usage of *iṣitam* is *chāndasa,* Vedic usage.

The mind is always objectifying one thing or the other. It is a *sādhāraṇaṁ karaṇam,* a common instrument of knowing, not an *asādhāraṇaṁ karaṇam,* a particular means. Eyes and so on are particular means for particular objects. Without the eyes, colour is not objectified, known. However, without the mind, eyes cannot see, ears cannot hear and so on. The mind is to be present in the perceptions of seeing, hearing, smelling, tasting, and touching. The mind includes also the *ahaṅkāra,* the I-sense; that is why the *ahaṅkāra* is not manifest when the mind goes to sleep.

If the mind itself is a *karaṇa,* a means, then there must be a *kartṛ,* a subject who employs the various means. The body-mind-sense complex is an assemblage, and its constituents are meant to serve, to function for someone different from the assembly, the one who is the subject.

Now, the question is, does the subject will the mind to do what it does? Since the mind can be directed deliberately in a given track of thinking there seems to be someone who wills. The mind not only objectifies the various objects, but also has desires for objects;

---

[9] इट्प्रयोगे सति गुणेन भवितव्यमिति (आनन्दगिरि)

When the suffix '*iṭ*' is added to the root '*iṣ*' the vowel '*i*' of the root '*iṣ*' has to take its *guṇa* form, '*e*'.

it responds to the objects and situations emotionally. The mind besides being able to recollect is also capable of reasoning and gaining certain knowledge—direct or indirect.

Does the subject will the activities of the mind? Or is it due to the mere presence of someone who himself does not will? The presence of the two verbs—*iṣitam* and *preṣitam* having a similar meaning—gives this alternative or extra sense.

Taking the word '*preṣitam*' first, let us suppose someone who wills, who impels the mind. Then, to have the will there should be a mind, because the will also is a thought-form subject to modification. That means you must have another mind to have a thought in the form of will. There is the defect of *anavasthā*, regression to infinity. The student is, therefore, not satisfied with the word '*preṣitam*' that he has used, and hence makes a change in the word sense by adding one more word, '*iṣitam*'.[10]

---

[10] संशयवतोऽयं प्रश्न इति प्रेषितशब्दस्य अर्थविशेष उपपद्यते। किं यथा प्रसिद्धमेव कार्यकरण-सङ्घातस्य प्रेषयितृत्वं किं वा सङ्घात-व्यतिरिक्तस्य स्वतन्त्रस्य इच्छामात्रेणैव मन-आदि-प्रेषयितृत्वं इत्यस्यार्थस्य प्रदर्शनार्थं केनेषितं पतति प्रेषितं मनः इति विशेषण-द्वयम् उपपद्यते। (केनभाष्यम्)

An additional meaning is tenable for the word *preṣita,* since the question comes from a student having doubt. Does the well known body-mind-sense complex itself engages into action or is there some other factor that is different from the assemblage and is independent that impels the mind etc., to function in their realm of operation by mere will? To point out this it is said *keneṣitaṁ patati preṣitaṁ manaḥ;* hence the use of two adjectives is tenable.

Kena iṣitam, sva-sannidhi-mātreṇa, manaḥ sva-viṣayeṣu patati: is there someone by whose mere presence, without a will, the mind and the senses function as such (who himself remains like a king)? The king by himself does not perform any task, but seated on the throne—wearing the crown, wielding the sceptre—he makes the whole kingdom active, the whole administration function.

A more germane example is the magnet. In the presence of a magnet the iron filings become active; they rush towards the magnet. The activity is created by the magnetic field by the mere presence of the magnet. Similarly, is there something inside me, which, without any will on its part, activates my mind to think of the various objects? What is the nature of the factor that is responsible for the mind to be mind, the senses to be senses?

The capacity of the mind to perceive things implies the presence of consciousness. If this is so, then, does the consciousness belong to the mind itself? Is the mind itself responsible for being conscious? Or is there any other principle that lights up the mind, making it capable of perception, knowing, desiring, willing, hearing, and so on? The mind and senses, being put-together, are meant to serve the purpose of someone else who is outside them. Is this 'someone' outside somewhere? If he is outside, where is he located? *Śāstra* alone has to reveal that.

We are going to see from the answer that the usage of both *preṣitam* and *iṣitam* are tenable. First the *śruti* will accept and answer the meaning of *iṣitam,* and later it will answer the meaning of *preṣitam.*

Kena prāṇaḥ prathamaḥ praiti yuktaḥ[11]: United with whom does the *prāṇa* perform its functions—breathing and other physiological activities? *Eti* means *gacchati*, moves, and *praiti* means methodically moves. *Prathamaḥ prāṇaḥ* means *mukhya-prāṇa*, the breath that makes one alive. *Prathamaḥ* does not mean first. Without the adjective *prathama*, *prāṇa* can mean *vāyu*, simple air. *Prāṇa* is *prathama* because without *prāṇa* the boasting senses cannot boast any more. The boasting person cannot talk. Even when the mind is not there, the *prāṇa* is there, as it happens in sleep. Only when there is *prāṇa*, is there the *jīva* indwelling the body. Life must be there in order to make something out of this body-mind-sense complex. Therefore, the *prāṇa* is called *prathamaḥ*.

In the *Bṛhadāraṇyakopaniṣad*, there is a story to illustrate the greatness of *prāṇa.* Once, all the organs that were disputing—who is the greatest among them, claiming, "I am great, I am great"—went to Brahmaji

---

[11] केन कर्त्रा युक्तः प्रयुक्तः प्रेरितः प्रथमः पञ्चवृत्यात्मकः प्राणः स्वविषयं प्रति प्रैति प्रकर्षेण एति गच्छति । (केनभाष्यम्)

United with which principle, the *mukhya-prāṇa* that is of five-fold nature methodically goes towards its functions.

for the verdict. Brahmaji said, "That organ is great on whose leaving, this body perishes." Each organ went out for one year and found, on its return, that everything was okay. When *prāṇa* began leaving, all the organs got uprooted and they all accepted the supremacy of *prāṇa*.

Kena satā yuktaḥ: being united with which existing principle that *mukhya-prāṇa* is *prāṇa* and does its job? Like even a pot. The pot is, because the clay is. Similarly, is the existence of *prāṇa* due to the existence of something else? *Praiti* means *ūrdhvaṁ gacchati*, goes up, meaning, one is able to breathe out and breathe in.

Kena iṣitām imāṁ vācaṁ vadanti (janāḥ): impelled by whom do people speak these words? *Imām* points out *prasiddha*, that which is well known. Is there something because of which people talk, making the organ of speech what it is? Being a conscious activity, the organ of speech has a particular function. It lights up all the objects for others' appreciation. Again, for the organ of speech to be, there should be certain knowledge involved, because it is put-together. Anything put-together presupposes knowledge. Therefore, is there a *sat*, a common conscious principle of existence, because of whose will the organ of speech performs its function?

Similarly, *cakṣuḥ śrotraṁ ka u devo yunakti*: which effulgent being makes the eyes and ears function?

The particle '*u*' has the meaning of *prasiddhi*, well-known status. The word *devaḥ* means *dyotanātmakaḥ*, the effulgent being.

The question indicates certain understanding on the part of the student. The very fact that he is asking the question shows he has *āpātata-jñāna*, certain understanding. Without any understanding there is no *jijñāsā*, desire to know. One does not desire for an unknown thing. Suppose, I say, "I am going to start a course on *gagabugain*." Nobody is going to apply for that. Even before desiring to know a topic, you must know something about it. Therefore, one cannot ask a question unless one has some knowledge; only then can one ask something more about it, or seek some clarity in what one knows already. Here, the student's knowledge is not complete; therefore he is asking a question.

Mantra 2

The answers to these questions and the ones that are asked later form this *upaniṣad* of Blessing.

श्रोत्रस्य श्रोत्रं मनसो मनो यद्
वाचो ह वाचं स उ प्राणस्य प्राणः ।
चक्षुषश्चक्षुरतिमुच्य धीराः
प्रेत्यास्माल्लोकादमृता भवन्ति ॥ १.२ ॥

śrotrasya śrotraṁ manaso mano yad
vāco ha vācaṁ sa u prāṇasya prāṇaḥ,
cakṣuṣaścakṣuratimucya dhīrāḥ
pretyāsmāllokād amṛtā bhavanti. (1.2)

śrotrasya – of the ear; *śrotram* – ear; *manasaḥ*– of the mind; *manaḥ* – mind; *yat* – which; *vācaḥ* – of the organ of speech; *ha* – indeed; *vācam*– organ of speech; *saḥ* – he; *u* – indeed; *prāṇasya* – of the breath; *prāṇaḥ* – the breath; *cakṣuṣaḥ*– of the eye; *cakṣuḥ* – eye; *atimucya* – freeing themselves; *dhīrāḥ* – the discriminative people; *pretya* – after leaving; *asmāt* – from this; *lokāt* – world; *amṛtāḥ* – immortal; *bhavanti* – become

It is indeed the self that is the ear of the ear, the mind of the mind, the speech of the speech, the breath of the breath and the eye of the eye. Those discriminative people, (who know the self), freeing themselves from this world (being free while living) are no more subject to death after leaving the body.

Śrotrasya śrotraṁ cakṣuṣaścakṣuḥ: Ear of the ear and eye of the eye. Here the word, '*śrotra*' appears in two different case endings. *Śrotrasya* is in the genitive case meaning 'of the ear' and *śrotram* is in the nominative case meaning 'ear'. So too, *cakṣuṣaścakṣuḥ*. *Cakṣuṣaḥ* means 'of the eye' and *cakṣuḥ* means 'eye'. From the answer we understand that the teacher is talking about the one reality that is both the ear of the ear and eye of the eye. The words '*sa u*' (he, indeed) also substantiates this. That which is presented in the genitive case is *asādhāraṇa*, uncommon, and the other, in the nominative case, is *sādhāraṇa*, common. The word 'ear' in the sixth case is *asādhāraṇa*, the particular instrument for hearing sound. The word 'ear' in the nominative case is *sādhāraṇa*, that is, the mind without which you cannot hear. So, *śrotrasya śrotram* is the mind, *cakṣuṣaścakṣuḥ* is also the mind. Therefore, it seems that the mind is the *ātman*, the *deva* that the student wanted to know.

On further inquiry, one recognises that the mind also is not *sādhāraṇa*—it differs from person to person, and even in a given person constantly moving from one state of experience to another. When we say it is not the mind, it means it is not a thought.

There seems to be one changeless *sādhāraṇa*, without which the mind is not mind, the eyes are not eyes, and the ears are not ears. Therefore, the teacher says, it is *manaso manaḥ*, the mind of the mind. The mind is *asādhāraṇa* and the *vastu* that is *sādhāraṇa*, is the mind of the mind. It is anybody's mind— the mind of a human being, of a mosquito, a cow, a monkey, and so on.

An objection may arise here. The student wanted to know if there is something in whose presence or by whose will the mind is mind, the senses are senses.

But the teacher seems to say something else. If the intention of the teacher is to present *ātman*, the consciousness, because of which the mind lands upon its objects, then, why does he not say it straightaway?

Suppose, the teacher says *ātman* is consciousness which is not the eyes, which is not the ears, which is not the mind; what will happen in the mind of the listener? That there is a consciousness that has to be realised. 'Realisation' is a new word brought in by certain people because they are not satisfied with the word 'knowledge'. For them realisation means the experience of a bliss that is projected as the final spiritual attainment. They call it enlightenment. The moment I say it is consciousness, immediately you will construe that it is something real, different from everything. Does it not imply that there are things and things, and one among them is consciousness? Then it becomes an object, different from the subject!

When I say, apple, banana, orange, monkey, and so on, you can understand the meaning of these words because they can be objectified. Now, suppose I say, 'consciousness.' What can you think about it? When you cannot think about it, how are you going to talk about it? That is why some say, 'It is beyond words.' The truth, however, is this: the invariable consciousness because of which you see, you hear; you are conscious of what is happening in your mind, you are conscious of anything, is self-revealing, self-evident.

The *śruti* here, therefore, purposely says: *śrotrasya śrotram*, ear of the ear. You need not search for that *deva*, the effulgent being. Then, why not we just say it is *śrotram*? No, because it is *cakṣuḥ*, eye, and it is also *manaḥ*, mind. Therefore, we have to say it is *śrotrasya śrotram*. That means you are never away from it. You see various objects, hear different sounds, know various thoughts taking place in your mind, because of the presence of consciousness in all of them. That is indeed what was asked for. It is the *sādhāraṇa*, the invariable presence, without which none of these exists.

The invariable presence is consciousness. The sound is, the sound consciousness is. Form is, form consciousness is. Thought is, thought consciousness is. Naturally, we say it is ear of the ear, eye of the eye, and mind of the mind. It is not that there is one more ear, a subtler one, for the organ of hearing. While it is neither the ear, nor the eye, nor the mind, one cannot merely say this because without that, there is no ear, there is no eye, and there is no thought either. There is no distance between the *vastu*, the reality, and any perception whatsoever; this is what the teacher wants to convey.

The invariable consciousness is not only with reference to perception, but also with reference to any action—talking or walking or eating. That without whose presence no perception or action is possible, is *nitya*, always present, and it is present everywhere.

In this understanding, the subject *ahaṅkāra*, 'I' thought, is swallowed; everything else is also swallowed. All the details are swallowed. Sometimes, the details have to be swallowed in order to see. Then, when you bring them back, your understanding stays in spite of details. The vision of the *śāstra* is just amazing.

That *vastu* which is behind the mind and senses and in whose presence the mind is mind, the senses are the senses, is the answer for the question, *kena iṣitam*. If the teacher says it differently, like "The *ātman* is the ear of the ear and so on," that will give room for implying the existence of *ātman* different from the senses and they are different from *ātman*. If it is said *śrotrasya śrotram*, the ear of the ear, then the real ear is not this sense organ called ear, but one without whom there is no ear at all. Further, *śrotrasya śrotram* also means that the ear of the ear is self-revealing. It makes all other sense organs what they are, without whose presence there would be no senses at all and without whose presence the mind itself would not exist.

The manner in which the teacher has answered has revealed two facts. One is, without the presence of the *vastu*, the senses cannot perform their cognitive tasks. That means it is invariably present in the variable.

In every cognition there is the presence of the *vastu,* the *caitanya,* consciousness.

The teacher need not give any other description about the *vastu* because the *vastu* is self-revealing. You cannot define consciousness; you need not define consciousness. It is only a word, and the meaning of the word is just 'you'.

When I say, 'consciousness,' it is not seen by you like a pot, tree and so on. It is not an object available for you to objectify, but at the same time, it is self-revealing self. That self-revealing consciousness which is present in the ear, eye, mind and so on, making them hear, see, think and so on, is the *śrotrasya śrotram, cakṣuṣaścakṣuḥ, manaso manaḥ*. So, the first fact revealed is that the ear, etc., are by themselves incapable of seeing; they have to be blessed by a conscious entity.

Another fact revealed by the statement *śrotrasya śrotram*, etc., is the 'existence aspect' of ears and so on. A thing is, it exists, because of consciousness that lends existence to it. *Śrotrasya śrotram* means that because of which *śrotra* is, *cakṣus* is, mind is, everything is. At the same time it itself is not a *śrotra*, etc. Here, that which is *śrotrasya śrotram* is also *cakṣusaścakṣuḥ.* The existence of the *śrotra* depends upon the same thing upon which the existence of the *cakṣus* depends, and so too the existence of the mind. What is invariably present is the *satya* and the differences in the form of *śrotra*, etc., are only apparent, *mithyā.* Thereby, there is no distance whatsoever between *śrotra*, etc., and the *ātman*.

What is revealed by this ingenious method of teaching is the self-revealing *atman* which is the only self-existent *vastu*, and it is you. The meaning of the word '*tvam,*' you, is unfolded in this *mantra*. This is purely *pratyagātma-siddhi*, arriving at what is the inner self.

There is a verse in the *Dakṣiṇāmūrti Stotram* unfolding this *pratyagātman* as consciousness through the analogy of beams of light.[12] Suppose, there is a pot with five holes and is kept inside a dark room with a bright lamp burning inside it. One can see five beams of light emanating from those holes. Each beam of light, lights up the objects falling in its way. Even though the beams are five in number, the light inside the pot and behind the five beams of light is only one. Similarly, each of the five sense organ lights up a given set of objects, but behind all of them there is only one consciousness. That consciousness behind the mind, behind the sense organs, is one and the same. There is nothing other than or behind consciousness. That consciousness is 'I', the *ātman*. The meaning of the

---

[12] नानाच्छिद्रघटोदरस्थितमहादीपप्रभाभास्वरं ज्ञानं यस्य तु चक्षुरादिकरणद्वारा बहिस्स्पन्दते... – whose consciousness illumines everything outside through the sense organs, such as eyes, like the light kept inside a pot having many holes, beaming out through them illumines objects (lying on the path of each beam). (*Dakṣiṇāmūrti Stotram*, Verse 4).

word 'I' can fall only in consciousness, it cannot be placed elsewhere.

When I see, I am the seer and when I hear, I am a hearer. It looks as though the 'I' is placed in the eye, in the ear because consciousness is very much present in the eyes, ears and so on. The whole physical body is a conscious entity with one sense organ, namely, the sense of touch that is present all over the physical body. Since consciousness is present in the physical body, it is possible to place the 'I' in the body. One can even take a thought also as 'I'. That is why one is restless when the mind is restless. This 'I' is placed in the mind because consciousness is present in every form of thought.

What is this 'I'? The meaning should necessarily resolve in consciousness. 'I' is without attributes, formless, simple consciousness alone. This is what the student wanted to know; that *vastu* as the impeller of the mind. *Śrotrasya śrotram* and so on is indeed the *ātman*.

Vāco ha vācam: It is the speech of the speech. Here, *vāk* should be taken only as the *śabda*, word. The second case ending in the word '*vācam*' should be converted into the nominative, *vāk*. It is *vācaḥ vāk*, the word of word, the cognition of the cognition. The meaning of a word is nothing but the cognition. The word 'pot' reveals an object. When the word is heard there is the recognition of its meaning. *Vāco ha vācam* refers to that because of which a word is heard and cognised, and which itself is not a word or its cognition. If it is a given cognition, then *ātman* is gone when that cognition is gone. This is not true. It is invariably present in every word—in the enunciation of every word, in pronunciation of every word, in the cognition of every word, in revealing an object through a word.*Ha* means indeed. *Vāk* stands for all the organs of action. That because of which the feet are feet, the hands are hands and the speech is speech, that which sustains all of them, giving reality to all of them, is the *vastu*. Both *sat*, existence and *cit*, cognition, are revealed here.

Sa u prāṇasya prāṇaḥ: He is indeed the *prāṇa* of the *prāṇa*. The *upaniṣad* changes the gender here. The same *vastu* is presented here in the masculine. All the genders are used because the *vastu* has no particular gender. This change of gender is deliberately done all the time in order to remove any gender orientation with regard to the self. The human mind, highly entrenched in gender, has to first get past this orientation.

If the self is neither male nor female it should not be construed as neuter. The self is free from all the three genders, while they are the self. Here, the *śāstra* quietly changes the gender; it started with *yat* which is *neuter*, then changed to *saḥ* which is masculine.

The same *vastu* alone is *prāṇasya prāṇaḥ*. The pronoun *saḥ*, he, is pointing out the same thing.

Prāṇa means that which makes the body alive, and which sustains this body. *Prāṇasya prāṇaḥ* is that *vastu* on which *prāṇa* itself is dependent for its existence and sustenance. The word '*prāṇa*' covers the other manifestations of *prāṇa* like *apāna*, *vyāna*, etc. When we say that *prāṇa* is, that 'is' is *prāṇasya prāṇaḥ*. All the three *śakti*s, capacities—*icchā-śakti*, the capacity to desire, *jñāna-śakti*, the capacity to know and *kriyā-śakti*, the capacity to do—are covered here, and all of them are dependent upon that one *vastu* which is *nirviśeṣa*, free from everything. Thus, nothing here in this body is left out as independent of that *vastu*.

We have to add here, *sa eva ātmā*—it is indeed the self. The *mantra* does not specifically mention this here because it is self-revealing. For instance, when you see me there is sight. Sight is defined as cognition of a form and colour. Hearing is cognition of sound and so on. The cognition is common. We can replace this word 'cognition' with 'consciousness' to say, form-consciousness, sound-consciousness, hunger-consciousness, doubt-consciousness, resolve-consciousness, memory-consciousness, time-consciousness, space-consciousness, the world-consciousness. In all these what is common is consciousness, *saṁvit*.

This invariable consciousness is *atman*. Where does one draw the line between the variable objects and the invariable consciousness? Can an object be separated from consciousness by an intervening 'object' like space? Or is the object itself included in that consciousness? If the object is always the same, then that one object becomes the attribute of consciousness. But that is not true; the objects are many and varied; they are variable. While objects depend upon consciousness, consciousness does not depend upon objects, nor does it have the objects as its attributes. Of the two, therefore, the variable object is *mithyā*, an incidental attribute, while the *vastu* is only one.

In order to account for the *jagat* the *śāstra* states, 'Brahman is the cause of everything.' The effect is *jagat*—all objects, known and unknown. This *jagat*, being a *kārya*, an effect, is shown as not separate from its cause, Brahman, and, therefore, it is *mithyā*. So, the object-consciousness is nothing but Brahman. Brahman is consciousness. When you add the object, it is consciousness, when you remove the object, then also it is consciousness. In fact, we really do not add or remove anything. The words *śrotrasya śrotram*, and so on, thus, lead to the *nirviśeṣa-vastu*, that which does not have the attribute of *śrotra*, etc. Here, the first *mantra* straightaway reveals that you are the self-revealing consciousness, invariably present in all situations.

Dhīrāḥ, the wise people, *atimucya*, having become free, *amṛtāḥ bhavanti*–are free from death. Since the words, '*dhīrāḥ*', and '*amṛtāḥ*' are mentioned, the word, '*jñātvā*, knowing'[13] is brought in by implication—knowing that *vastu* which is *śrotrasya śrotram*, etc., *dhīrāḥ*, the wise people become free from death. Later, this *vastu* is going to be further revealed as Brahman. But in the first *mantra*, the *śāstra* presents the result of this knowledge, namely, *amṛtatva*, immortality.

In the *Kaṭhopaniṣad*, there is an appropriate *mantra* that is relevant here for our study. It says: *parāñci khāni vyatṛṇat svayambhūstasmāt parāṅ paśyati nāntarātman kaścit dhīraḥ pratyagātmānam aikṣat āvṛtta-cakṣuḥ amṛtatvam icchan* (2.1).[14] The sense organs for this *jīva* are externalised naturally. Suppose, the Lord internalised all of them, then one will always be seeing what is going on inside the body and feel permanently sick. Further, the world created by the Lord that is available for public appreciation will become

---

[13] प्रष्टुः पृष्टस्यार्थस्य ज्ञातुमिष्टत्वात् श्रोत्रादेः श्रोत्रादिलक्षणं यथोक्तं ब्रह्म ज्ञात्वा इत्यध्याह्रियते। अमृताः भवन्ति इति फलश्रुतेश्च। ज्ञानात् हि अमृतत्वं प्राप्यते। (केनभाष्यम्)

Since the student desires to know what he has asked for, the word 'having known' is brought in, meaning, 'knowing Brahman that has been unfolded as the ear of the ear' etc. Also, because there is the *śruti-vākya* 'they become free from death' mentioning the result. Indeed, freedom from death is attained only by knowledge.

[14] The Lord created the sense organs externalised and thereby (seems to have) destroyed the *jīva*. Therefore, everyone looks out and does not see the inner self. A rare wise person, desiring freedom and turning inward, sees the self.

redundant. The world is meant for experience and to exhaust one's *karma*. Therefore, the world of objects is there and to objectify them, the senses are made external.

One may think that the Lord seems to have destroyed this *jīva* by making the senses external. The Lord provided these senses to the *jīva* to objectify and transact with the world and thereby help himself. The *jīva* does perceive the sense objects through the given set of senses, but looks upon the objects as separate from him, and himself as someone separate from them. *Antarātmānaṁ na paśyati*—he does not understand that there is someone 'behind' the subject and the object, who is the eye of the eye, the ear of the ear, the mind of the mind, and so on. When it is said that it is the mind of the mind, all three, *jñātṛ-jñāna-jñeya,* the cogniser, the cognition and the cognised object, are included. No knowledge of any object takes place without the relevant object being present in the knowledge. Any knowledge implies the presence of the knower too. All three have their basis in the invariable *caitanya* which is referred here as *antarātman.*

Why does the individual not see the *antarātman*? Because he takes the body, senses and the mind themselves as the *ātman,* and looks at everything else as *anātman*, other than himself. Therefore, *parāṅ paśyati,* he looks out all the time.

Among the *jīva*s, there is someone who is a *dhīra*, a wise man, who clearly sees the *atman* as the ear of the ear, and so on. *Aikṣat*, he saw, he recognised. The wise man clearly sees the difference between *pratyak* and *parāk*, inner and external, and also sees the non-difference. He recognises that it is the self because of which all these exist, and from whom they are non-separate.

How did the wise man recognise the self? Because he is *āvṛtta-cakṣu*, the one who recognises the one *vastu* behind the eyes, ears, mind and so on; not by withdrawing the senses, but by understanding the truth behind them. He gains this knowledge, desiring freedom, *amṛtatvam icchan*.

'Desiring freedom,' does not imply that it is optional. Seeing this fact that it is not optional is called *puruṣārtha-niścaya*; clearly understanding the human goal. So a *dhīra* recognises the *ātman*. This *upaniṣad* also talks about the same *dhīra*. It is amazing to see this *samanvaya*, connection, in all the *upaniṣad*s—all of them talk about the same truth, the same vision, in the same language; there is not even a dash bit of difference. The very *śravaṇa* is meant to see non-difference in all these things.

Pretya asmāllokād amṛtāḥ bhavanti: they gain freedom from death after leaving this body. They are free from *saṁsāra*. Two expressions are used here: *atimucya* and *asmād lokāt pretya*. *Atimucya* means giving up the notion of 'I' in the ears,[15] etc. In all of them I have *ātma-buddhi*, the understanding that I am all of them, and *ātmīya-buddhi*, the knowledge that they are all attributes that belong to and depend upon me. In fact, the attributes do not belong to me at all. I am free from ears, even though the ears are not free from me. This difference has to be seen very clearly. They are subject to time; I am not. I am the *ātman* and the *ātman* of every being and every thing.

Pretya asmāllokāt means[16] dying to the notion that I am as good as the body. *Asmāt* means from this. 'This' is a pronoun that stands for something that is known very well. The literal meaning of *asmād lokāt* will be from this *loka*, this world of experience. But here, in the context, *loka*[17] means the *kārya-karaṇa-saṅghāta*, physico-physio-psycho complex, that which every individual does know very well. The physical body is called the *kārya* and the subtle body that makes this body function is called *karaṇa*. Having understood this, the wise person has withdrawn the 'I' from this assemblage.

---

[15] श्रोत्रादौ आत्मभावं परित्यज्य। (केन भाष्यम्)
Giving up the notion of 'I' in the ears etc.

[16] सर्वप्राणिप्रत्यक्षाद् लोकात् कार्यकरणसङ्घाताभिमानाद् इत्यर्थः।
It means 'from the notion that I am the body-mind-(sense)-complex that is directly perceived by all the beings'.

[17] लोक्यते दृश्यते अनुभूयते इति लोकः।
That which is seen, experienced, is called *loka*.

Withdrawal is not enlightenment. In sleep even though the *kārya-karaṇa-saṅghāta*, the body-mind-sense complex, is withdrawn, one does not wake up enlightened! *Vyāvṛtya*, dying, means giving up, in terms of knowledge; that is why the word *dhīrāḥ*, has been used. The wise people having known—'I am *śrotrasya śrotraṁ manaso mano yat, vāco ha vācam,*'—*amṛtāḥ bhavanti*, are no longer subject to death. They gain freedom from death, mortality.

What is subject to death, dies. This physical body is subject to death because it is a put-together assemblage, subject to disintegration. A house, a cell, a nucleus, or anything being put-together entities, does not remain in the same form. If one's 'I' is as good as the physical body, one is a mortal. A wise person's 'I' is placed in *śrotrasya śrotram*, that which has no particular form, that which is not an assembly, and which is not made up of parts—and which is *caitanya*, consciousness. Naturally, these wise people are free.

That the body dies is not a problem. That 'I die' is the problem. That the body is ugly is not a problem, that 'I am ugly' is the problem. That the body is fat is not a problem, that 'I am fat' is the problem. The attributes of the body, mind, and senses are taken to be the 'I' and I suffer. Freedom from suffering is freedom from the notions about the 'I' that cause suffering.

Śāstra uses the words, *atimucya* and *asmāllokāt pretya*, to convey two different ideas here. *Atimucya dhīrāḥ amṛtāḥ bhavanti*—giving up the *ātma-buddhi*, the I-notion, in the ears, eyes, mind, etc., and thereby releasing the *ātman* from all the wrong notions—the wise people gain immortality. *Prāṇasya prāṇaḥ* does not give up its breath. There is no last breath or first breath for the self. So, what is meant here is only giving up the notion that 'I' is all of them.

Will the wise people come back again after death? Each wise person is the same Brahman. There is no coming back for Brahman. The wise people know they are Brahman, and so there is no coming back for them either. There is no other person available there to come back. Therefore, *asmāllokāt pretya*, leaving this physical body, they do not come back. This has to be pointed out because the *śāstra* talks about *loka-prāpti*, attainment of various realms of experience, like *svarga*, Vedic heaven and *punar-janma*, rebirth, for all *jīvas*, in keeping with their *karmas*. It has presented a model of *karma*. Naturally, the same *śāstra* has to release the *jīva* from the spell of *karma*. That this release from *karma*, and *mokṣa* is possible is presented here saying that there is no coming back for the wise; they have released the *ātman* from the body-mind-sense complex in their cognition–that the *ātman* is Brahman.

Atimucya refers to *jīvanmukti* and *asmāllokāt pretya amṛtāḥ bhavanti* refers to absence of rebirth.

Their *prāṇa*s do not proceed further on the fall of the body, but all resolve here.[18] This is an expression of the *śāstra*, to make one understand that *ātman* is always free from *karma.* First it tells, *ātman* is subject to *karma,* and, therefore, one is answerable for one's *puṇya-pāpa* as long as one is a *kartṛ,* doer. One does not escape from it. Later, when one comes to know the nature of the *ātman,* which one must know, then one is free from birth and death, because all the *karma*s get falsified.[19]

This *mantra* tells all that is to be told in a brief manner. Then it also explains the meaning and its style. What is *śrotrasya śrotram* is not said. The *upaniṣad* is very confident that one will recognise it as the invariable in every cognition, because it is self-revealing and explains why it is saying so. Therefore there is no random expression here—it is a way of conscious communication to make sure one does not go away with any wrong idea. The *upaniṣad* now explains why it is adopting this particular method of unfoldment.

---

[18] न तस्य प्राणाः उत्क्रामन्ति (बृहदारण्यक 4.4.6)

Their *prāṇa* does not leave (this body).

[19] क्षीयन्ते चास्य कर्माणि तस्मिन् दृष्टे परावरे (मुण्डक 2.2.9)

When that Brahman, which is in the form of cause and effect is recognised, all his *karma*s get exhausted.

Mantra 3

The student asked a straightforward question, "Is there some one behind these eyes, ears...?" But the teacher is giving a round about answer. On the contrary, the teacher should have answered, "Yes, there is someone behind the eyes, ears, etc., who is of this description." Instead he says, "*śrotrasya śrotram, manaso mano yat*," and so on. Thus, a question naturally arises as to why the teacher does not reveal the *vastu* straightaway as 'this,'[20] like even one would reveal a pot by pointing out the object and say, "This is pot." This question is answered now.

न तत्र चक्षुर्गच्छति न वाग्गच्छति नो मनो
न विद्मो न विजानीमो यथैतदनुशिष्यात्।
अन्यदेव तद्विदितादथो अविदितादधि
इति शुश्रुम पूर्वेषां ये नस्तद्व्याचचक्षिरे ॥ १.३ ॥

na tatra cakṣurgacchati na vāggacchati no mano na vidmo na vijānīmo yathaitad anuśiṣyād, anyadeva tadviditād atho aviditād adhi iti śuśruma pūrveṣāṁ ye nastad vyācacakṣire. (1.3)

na – not; *tatra* – there; *cakṣuḥ* – eye; *gacchati* – goes; *na* – not; *vāk* – organ of speech; *gacchati*– goes; *na u* – not indeed; *manaḥ* – mind; *na* – not; *vidmaḥ* – we know (Brahman) as an object;

---

20 इदन्तया किं न प्रदश्यते । Why it is not pointed out as 'this'.

na – not; *vijānīmaḥ* – we know; *yathā* – how; *etad* – this; *anuśiṣyāt* – would be taught; *anyat* – different; *eva* – only; *tad* – that; *viditāt* – from the known; *atha u* – also; *aviditāt* – from the unknown; *adhi* – different; *iti* – thus; *śuśruma*– we heard; *pūrveṣām* – of the predecessors; *ye*– who; *naḥ*– to us; *tat* – that; *vyācacakṣire*– expounded

Eyes have no access there. The organ of speech (also) does not reach there, nor does the mind. We do not recognise it as an object. We do not (therefore) know how to impart this knowledge (in any other way). It is indeed different from the known and also from the unknown. Thus, we have heard from (our) predecessors who expounded it to us.

Na tatra cakṣurgacchati: Eyes do not reach there. *Tatra* means *tasmin ātmani*, with reference to the *ātman*. The eye does not go there; it is not the object of sight. *Na gacchati* means *na prāpnoti*, it does not objectify (the *ātman*).

Suppose I say, *ātman* has this particular form that resembles a pumpkin. The eyes can objectify because pumpkin has a form that one can see. Then one could easily say that *ātman* is like a pumpkin. One has knowledge of a given form because the eyes have access to that form. If one does not have the knowledge of a particular form, then one can always bring in a similar thing that one knows, and with that one can point out the thing to be known. For instance, if you do not know what a 'laddu' is, I can describe it by saying, it is a sweet that looks like a ping-pong ball, is yellow in colour, has a granular finish, and breaks when pressed. Now, I have made you informed enough to know what a 'laddu' is like. If I give you a 'laddu', you will recognise it because of the description you already have. This is how we communicate things. If the person does not know what a ping-pong ball is, or what yellow is, and so on, it is difficult to communicate. A reference frame is a must in the person with whom one communicates. Based upon that reference frame alone, one can communicate things that can be communicated.

Here, what is the reference frame that one has to point out *ātman*? If it has a particular form, then it can be described. What we are talking about is something that is the eye of the eye. Therefore, it is not an object for the eyes. Being free from form, it is not available for the eyes to objectify. Anything that one objectifies through the eyes will be dissimilar to what is being talked about. Is this not true? Since the eyes have no access to the *ātman,* then any form one picks up by operating the eyes is irrelevant in making one appreciate the *ātman*.

Maybe the organ of speech has access to it. For instance, heaven, to which the eyes have no access, can be known through words. One can go to any place in this world and see what it is all about, but not to heaven. Even if the eyes do not have access to heaven, I can still describe about heaven through words and give some indirect knowledge about it. One can believe it and wait for heaven after death. Where the sense organs do not dare, the words can dare to go. Therefore, words can, perhaps, say how the *vastu* is. No.

Na vāg gacchati: The word also does not go there. Why? It is the *ātman* of the word, because of which the word is a word;[21] already it was pointed out as *vāco ha vācam*. If we take the meaning of *vāk* as the organ of speech, it will ultimately mean the word that is spoken by the organ of speech. Therefore, words are not going to objectify the *ātman*.

A given word can reveal any of the following: a *jāti*, species; *guṇa*, quality of an object; a *kriyā*, action, and *sambandha*, relationship of an object with something else. A word like 'pot' reveals an object that excludes *vijāti*, every other object belonging to any other species in the world. There are many objects in the world unlike the pot, like table, chair and so on. All these objects are excluded by this word 'pot'. Among the pots too, this is only a single pot.

---

21 शब्दस्य तन्निर्वर्तकस्य च करणस्य आत्मा ब्रह्म । अतो न वाग्गच्छति । (केनभाष्यम्)

Brahman is the *ātman*, the content of the word and the instrument that manifests the word and hence word does not reach there.

Therefore, objects belonging to the same species also are excluded by the word 'pot'. It reveals only a *vyakti*, object, and that is a given pot. If you say it is a brown pot, then the word 'brown' dismisses a black pot and so on. Further, a pot has many limbs like the neck, the stomach and so on. Words can be used to describe the pot with reference to its limbs. Similarly, the word 'father' or 'son' reveals the relationship of a given person with another related person. A word like 'cook' can reveal the person with reference to his action. The name of a person or an object can be revealed by a word, like Rāma; that is a proper noun. These are the capacities of words.

Now, which is the word that can be used to reveal this *ātman*? If everything that is here is *ātman*, then one has to repeat the entire dictionary in all the languages in order to indicate the *ātman*. Even a Sanskrit dictionary is always incomplete, as it does not include compounds. Compounds are created at will by the author at the time of writing. So, the words are infinite in Sanskrit because one can invent new words using the existing language. One has to cover all the words, in all the dialects, and in all the languages to reveal the *ātman*.

Even if we include all the words in order to reveal *ātman*, we always have to keep adding more because we have words only for things that are known to us. But there are plenty of unknown things. In fact, they are numerous than the known things and they are all Brahman! By which word are we going to cover those unknown things?

Again, which is that word that can reveal the *ātman*'s pure nature, that is, without any *nāma-rūpa,* name and form? If I ask you what *ātman* is, you have to keep quiet, for you cannot use any word; every word is nothing but a name and form.

Suppose, we use the word, '*satya*' and say *ātman* is *satya*. The word '*satya*' does not reveal anything except that it is not a non-existent entity. By negation, the word serves only as a *lakṣaṇa,* a word whose meaning is by implication. It is not just the word meaning.

Words do have their limitations. Verbally, the *vastu* cannot be talked about as an object. There are not many *ātmans*. So, *ātman* cannot be pointed out as a *jāti*. There is no *guṇa,* either, for *ātman*. A *guṇa* is an attribute of an object and which can be objectified. If you see an attribute in *ātman,* then it becomes an object, enjoying the attribute. There is no attribute without a locus, and unless you objectify that locus you are not going to see the attribute. To see the white cow, you should see the cow; only then will you see the whiteness also. So, *ātman* being not an object there is no attribute either. Already by the words *śrotrasya śrotraṁ manaso mano yat* etc., the teacher has dismissed the object-status for *ātman*.

Ātman has no *sambandha* either. What is the *sambandha* between *satya* and *mithyā*? All relationships are between objects obtaining in the same order, sphere of reality. For instance, there is no *sambandha* between a dream mansion and the waker living in a rented flat. *Sambandha* is not possible between two objects enjoying dissimilar degrees of reality. The waking reality is different from the dream reality. *Ātman* being *satya,* and everything else being *mithyā,* dependent upon that *ātman,* there is no *sambandha* for *ātman*—just as between the pot and clay there is no *sambandha*. Pot is clay. There is no *kriyā* in *ātman,* for it does not perform any action—*kurvannapi na karoti,* it does not do in spite of doing. *Ātman* is free from action.

How are you going to talk about the *ātman* that is not subject to species, attributes, actions and connections? Because of this impossibility it has been said: *mauna-vyākhyā-prakaṭita-para-brahma-tatvam...,*[22] the truth that is the limitless Brahman is revealed by silence. This sentence has to be understood correctly. Nothing is revealed by silence, unless one interprets the silence correctly. If silence is the language, then it requires to be interpreted. If you ask me a question and I remain silent, that silence can be interpreted in a hundred different ways; it all depends upon one's emotional make up. The silence can reveal

---

22 *Dakṣiṇāmūrti Dhyāna-śloka*

my ignorance too. I may have no clue about how to answer the question; therefore I may be silent. Or, my silence may mean that I am asking you to think for yourself; why should I worry about it? Or, it may mean that I have answered it any number of times, and do not want to repeat myself. So, silence does not communicate anything particular.

Why can't we interpret silence as *ātman*? No. Noise also is *ātman*. *Sarvaṁ khalvidaṁ brahma,*[23] all that is here is Brahman that is *ātman*. If you say that you interpret *ātman* from the silence, then that means you have the knowledge of *ātman*. If you have knowledge of *ātman*, then you do not require interpreting anybody's silence. Therefore, when it is said that *ātman* is revealed by silence, it means that *ātman* is not the immediate meaning of any word.

There are particular words that reveal after negation, retaining their own *dhātvartha*, root meaning. For instance, the root meaning of the word '*satya*' is existence; so 'is' is the meaning. But at the same time, the *vastu* does not exist in time. The word '*satya*' negates the limitation in existence. It is in grammatical apposition to the word *ananta* by which you can understand its meaning.

In order to conform to the word *ananta*, naturally, the word *satya* has to give up its meaning of limited

[23] *Chāndogyopaniṣad* 3.14.1

existence, of being existent in time. Therefore, the word '*satya*' is taken as the *lakṣyārtha,* the implied meaning alone, and not *vācyārtha,* the immediate meaning of the word. Hence it is said, *na vāg gacchati*. People do ask, "If words have no access, why are you talking, why are we studying, and what for is this *śāstra*?" We have to know the role of the words in revealing the *ātman*.

Where the words do not go, the mind at least can go. Goddess Sarasvatī, being omniscient, has all disciplines of knowledge. There is no piece of knowledge that is unknown to her. Suppose I ask her, "Mother! Tell me what is the difference in taste between honey and sugarcane juice?" She will only smile and say, "Taste both of them separately and find out for yourself." Even for Goddess Sarasvatī the difference between the two tastes is not a matter for verbal communication. You can understand the difference only by the sense of taste and the mind. Certain things can be understood only with the mind. Emotions like love and so on can be seen in the mind; one is able to appreciate it, though one cannot fully express it. Love is a particular frame of mind that obtains when the mind is resolved and assumes a cheerful disposition because the object perceived is highly pleasing to you. Though not available for much verbal communication, love can be appreciated purely with the mind.

Perhaps here also, the *vastu*—though not available for sensory objectification or any verbal communication—is available for me to appreciate with my mind. The teacher says, "No."

Na u manaḥ: Not even the mind. Neither does the mind go there. Then why do you talk about it? What cannot be understood by the mind can never be understood at all. No, it is not so. What is said here is that the mind cannot comprehend it as an object. For instance, the pot is not going to objectify the clay of which it is made. The clay is the very subject, the very content of the pot, and hence the clay is not available for the pot to objectify. Similarly, *ātman*, the content of the very thought is not available for objectification by the thought itself. Therefore, *manaḥ na gacchati*. The mind can objectify everything else, but not Brahman, the content of itself.[24]

Every thought is momentary. If *ātman* is an object of a given thought, it will be replaced by another thought, a chair thought, for instance. The *ātman* thought will be gone when the chair thought comes and the chair thought will be gone if some other thought comes. There will be no difference between

---

[24] नो मनः। मनश्चान्यस्य सङ्कल्पयितृ अध्यवसायितृ च सद् नात्मानं सङ्कल्पयति अध्यवस्यति च। तस्यापि ब्रह्म आत्मेति। (केनभाष्यम्)

Not mind. Mind that thinks and ascertains about those that are different from itself, cannot think or ascertain about itself. Brahman is the *ātman*, the content of the mind itself.

the chair and the *ātman*. You are always *ātman*. What we call 'always,' is the *ātman*. We are dealing with the infinite, not any finite object. So, *na vāg gacchati, na u manaḥ*.

Na vidmaḥ: We do not know. Without being taught in this manner—*śrotrasya śrotram, cakṣuṣaścakṣuḥ, manaso manaḥ*—we cannot know the *vastu* through the various means of knowledge, such as perception, inference and so on, at our disposal. The *guru* says '*na vidmaḥ,*' a plural word, meaning 'we do not know,' identifying with his predecessors. He clearly knows; already he has said *śrotrasya śrotram*. Then, what does he mean by saying, "We do not know?" The *guru* reveals that the *vastu* is not an object of the eyes, the ears, and so on, muchless it is object of a thought.[25] Therefore, *na vidmaḥ*, we do not see it as one of the objects. Unlike any other object, it is to be recognised differently. That is why it was said *śrotrasya śrotraṁ manaso mano yat*. Since it is self-revealing we do not require saying anything more.

Everything is, because I am self-evident, self-revealing consciousness. I am consciously seeing an object, and I am consciously hearing a sound.

---

25 इन्द्रिय-मनोभ्यां हि वस्तुनो विज्ञानम्। तदगोचरत्वान्न विद्मः तद् ब्रह्म ईदृशमिति। (केनभाष्यम्)

By both senses and the mind, indeed, knowledge of (any) object takes place. Being not objectified by them, we do not know 'that Brahman is in this form.'

Consciousness is the *vastu* because of which the form-consciousness is, the sound-consciousness is, or any thought-consciousness is. That is the reason why there is no other way of presenting it.

Na vijānīmaḥ yathā etad anuśiṣyāt: We do not know in which manner a teacher (like me) would teach this *vastu* to a disciple like you.[26] In no other manner can we teach the *vastu* except by revealing it as the eye of the eye, ear of the ear and so on.

Why do you say so? Because what I am talking about is *anidaṁ rūpaṁ vastu*. *Idam* means 'this'. *Anidam* means that which is not subject to become 'this'. It is not something that can be referred as 'this' object, opposed to the subject. It is the content of both the subject and object. It has no particular *viśeṣa*, attribute; so it cannot be described like a pot.

Further, the teacher says, "We understood the *vastu* because this is how we were taught. We are teaching you in the same way." This is the *sampradāya*, the tradition of teaching.

The teacher gives a reason for this method of teaching. *Tat anyad eva viditād atho aviditād adhī*: That (what was said as *śrotrasya śrotram*...) is above

---

[26] न विजानीमो यथा येन प्रकारेण एतद् ब्रह्म अनुशिष्याद् उपदिशेत् शिष्याय इत्यभिप्रायः। (केनभाष्यम्)

We do not know in which manner (a teacher like me) would teach this Brahman to a disciple (like you).

what is known and unknown. *Vidita* is known, that which is available as an object of perception, inference and so on. That which is not known is called *avidita*. You can only objectify what is known to you. *Ātman* is other than that because it is not an 'object' of your knowledge, of your means of knowledge. Then, it becomes what is *avidita*, not known. Does it mean *ātman* is unknown? No. It is other than what is unknown also, being not away from you; it is you.

Anything created has a distinct form and attribute that can be known, because those features are available for knowing through some means of knowledge or the other.[27] It has the status of knowability. Therefore, a *kārya*, effect, can be called *vidita*, known now or later.

Ātman is *viditād adhi*, it is not a *kārya*, a created thing. Perhaps it is *kāraṇa*, material cause. He says, *aviditāt adhi*. *Avidita* is *kāraṇa*. It is other than the material cause also. The material cause undergoes a process of change to become the creation. *Ātman* does not undergo any process of change to become this creation, like even the rope does not undergo any change to become the cause for the perception of snake. The creation is apparent and is not independent of its cause, the *vastu*. A rope-snake cannot appear without the rope giving existence to the snake.

---

27 सर्वमेव व्याकृतं विदितमेव । (केन भाष्यम्).

All that is manifest is indeed 'known'.

Any effect, creation, 'is' and that 'is-ness' belongs to *ātman* alone. Since *ātman* does not undergo any change whatsoever, we cannot really say *ātman* is the cause of creation. So, it is neither an effect nor the cause. *Adhi* means *adhikam*. It is something that is above. It is above the known, the *kārya*, the effect, and it is above the unknown, the *kāraṇa*, the cause.

If *ātman* is something caused, that means it arrives at a given time. If it arrives at a given time, then you are already there to know the arrival of the *ātman*. But, *ātman* neither arrives nor departs. It does not have a beginning or an end. Cause and effect are not two different things. From one standpoint *ātman* is effect, and from another standpoint, cause. *Ātman* is neither cause nor an effect. The *caitanya*, consciousness, gives existence and reality to both cause and effect. That *caitanya* is you, *ātman*. In any way you look at, it just resolves in you, the *ātman*.

The whole world is nothing but known plus unknown. The unknown part is always greater than the known part. A given object, like a flower for instance, is known as well as unknown. One may know a rose flower but one does not know why it is red in colour. One knows a person, but does not know what are all his or her problems. Also with reference to one's own body one knows something, but does not know many things. Even with reference to one's own mind one cannot always know its ways.

For instance, the unconscious is part of the mind, and it is not known to many of us. Therefore, nobody knows the entire mind of oneself or of anybody.

The teacher says, the *ātman*, you, is more than the known and unknown. How is that? What transcends both known and unknown cannot be an object because both known and unknown are only with reference to objects. What is above known and unknown is just *ātman*, you. There is no way of missing it. Therefore, both known and unknown are non-separate from the *ātman*. That means you are the very knowledge because of which you know what you know, and you know what you do not know. That is the *vastu* and therefore you have no problem of ignorance.

The problem is not centred on the intellect or the mind or the body. It is centred on 'I'. That 'I' is already free from being ignorant and informed. The self is already free. Thus, those people who taught us, taught us in this manner alone. There is no other way to teach. In any other way also, one has to negate what one is not. *Śrotrasya śrotram* means one negates the variable—the eyes, ears, nose, etc.—and understands the invariable presence of consciousness behind them, that makes them what they are.

In this expression '*anyad eva tad viditād atho aviditād adhi*' one cannot commit the mistake of imposing any kind of conditioning, or forming any concept about the *ātman*. This is the method of teaching. Suppose, I say, *ātman* is eternal, immortal and so on. Any mind will project an eternity that may be opposed to time, but, nevertheless, it will be a projection based upon the concept of finite time. On this finite concept one projects the infinite, or something that is the opposed to finite. It is again a concept.

The tendency of the mind is to jump from one concept to another; it hardly gives that up. That is how we divide our life into bits. When the word 'spiritual' is used, one immediately makes a division saying, this is material, and that is spiritual, even though there is no material or spiritual division as such. If you analyse, all that is material is nothing but spiritual. And again, all that is spiritual is material. If the mind gives up one thing, it holds on to the opposite or some other thing. Naturally, the teacher, while communicating, has to take into account this tendency of the mind and communicate the *vastu* that is formless, free from attributes, and yet has all the attributes of the creation because there is nothing that is away from it.

The problem here is, if one says that *ātman* is 'this,' then the mind excludes everything else. If *ātman* is said to be mind of the mind, then immediately one concludes that there exists another thing that is beyond thoughts, independent of thoughts, and so on. Hence, if *ātman* is to be known as it is, then it has to be conveyed in a manner where no mistake can be committed. When I say, *ātman* is neither known nor unknown, it is you; you cannot take it as anything else, not even as a simple thought. So, the teacher says, this is how we were taught.

Iti śuśruma pūrveṣāṁ ye nastad vyācacakṣire: Thus, we have heard from our predecessors who expounded it to us. How? *Anyadeva tad viditād atho aviditād adhi*, it is indeed different from the known and the unknown. In this manner alone we heard, we understood and we teach the same way. May you also understand it the same way; there is no other way.

The usage of the first person plural is to identify with all the teachers who have gone before. Who are these teachers? He says, *ye nastad vyācacakṣire*, those well-versed in the *śāstra* who taught us that *vastu* until we understood.[28] So, those teachers taught until the truth was understood; that is the teaching tradition. It is not mysticism based on some experience. Where experience is involved, there is no tradition involved, and no communication possible. Experience is to be understood, assimilated. Here, the knowledge assimilated is communicable, totally. The prefixes *vi* and *ā* in *vyācacakṣire* are, therefore, significant in this regard. *Tat* means that *vastu*, which is pointed by the words *śrotrasya śrotraṁ manaso mano yat* and so on.

---

[28] ये आचार्याः नः अस्मभ्यं ब्रह्म व्याचचक्षिरे व्याख्यातवन्तः विस्पष्टं कथितवन्तः तेषाम् इत्यर्थः । (केनभाष्यम्) – 'Those teachers who taught us (*naḥ*) clearly *brahma*,' this is the meaning.

Mantra 4

Further,

यद्वाचानभ्युदितं येन वागभ्युद्यते ।
तदेव ब्रह्म त्वं विद्धि नेदं यदिदमुपासते ॥ १.४ ॥

yad vācānabhyuditaṁ yena vāg abhyudyate,
tad eva brahma tvaṁ viddhi nedaṁ yad idam upāsate. (1.4)

yat – that; *vācā* – by speech; *anabhyuditam*– not revealed; *yena* – by which; *vāk* – the speech; *abhyudyate* – is revealed; *tad* – that; *eva* –alone; *brahma* – Brahman; *tvam* – you; *viddhi* – know; *na* – not; *idam* – this; *yat* – which; *idam* – (as) 'this'; *upāsate* – (people) worship

May you know that alone to be Brahman, which is not revealed by speech (but) by which speech is revealed, and not this that people worship (as an object).

The first line reveals primarily the *pratyagātman*, the inner self, that which is ear of the ear, etc., that which is neither known nor unknown, but the basis of both the known and the unknown. In the second line the inner self is pointed out as Brahman by saying *tadeva brahma tvaṁ viddhi,* may you understand that is Brahman.

While *Chāndogya Upaniṣad* says, "*tat tvam asi,* that (Brahman) you are," here, the teacher says, "*tad eva brahma tvaṁ viddhi,* may you understand that alone to be Brahman." That 'you,' is the eye of the eye, ear of the ear, etc., and which is neither the known nor the unknown. All these details make the meaning of *tat* very clear; it is you. Understand that consciousness alone to be Brahman which is you, in whose presence you are aware of all these things. Brahman means limitless, the cause of everything—that from which everything has come, and unto which everything goes back. You are that Brahman.

Yad vācā anabhyuditam: That which is not revealed by the word. *Anabhyuditam means na prakāśitam,*[29] not objectified by a word. The *vastu* is not revealed as the direct meaning of any word. It is unlike the object 'pot' that is revealed by the word 'pot'. However, the *vastu* is revealed by words through implication, after creating a context.

Yena vāg abhyudyate: By whose presence a word comes to manifest. Here, we have to take into account all that is connected to a word—by whose presence alone a word is a word, a word is pronounced as a word, a word is heard, a word is understood. In the presence of the invariable *pratyagātman* alone a word is heard and its meaning understood. So too, it comes to manifest.

The word '*vāk*' can also be taken to mean the organ of speech. That *caitanya*, consciousness, which the

---

29 अनभ्युदितम् अप्रकाशितम् । (केनभाष्यम्). Not revealed.

organ of speech cannot objectify, but because of which it is able to function, is Brahman.[30] This meaning is given here because a story is going to be narrated later, based upon this fact.

That *vastu* which is not revealed by a word, but because of which a word comes to manifest, is referred by the word, '*tat*' which, in the context of the previous unfoldment, means 'you'. The *mantra* exhorts you to understand *tad vastu*, that *caitanya*, to be Brahman.

The word Brahman is already arrived at in the language. It is derived from the root *bṛh*,[31] in the sense of growth. *Bṛhatvād brahma*, that which is big or *bṛhmaṇāt brahma*, that which is capable of growing into *jagat*. Both meanings are applicable here. The bigness here is *aparicchinna*, unrestricted. Hence, Brahman is *ananta* that which is limitless—time-wise or space-wise.

An object is limited both in terms of space and time—previously it was not, now it is. Whereas, Brahman is unlike any object that exists in time and space. Space itself is *paricchinna*, limited. Even though

---

[30] येन ब्रह्मणा विवक्षिते अर्थे सकरणा वाग् अभ्युद्यते चैतन्यात्मज्योतिषा प्रकाश्यते प्रयुज्यते इति । (केनभाष्यम्)

By which Brahman, the light of consciousness, the word along with the means, is employed, revealed, in the desired area of communication.

[31] *bṛhi (bṛṁh) vṛddhau* to grow (Root number 1136 of *dhātupāṭha*).

space is relatively all-pervasive, it does not pervade Brahman. In fact, Brahman pervades space. That is why space is part of the *jagat*. Therefore, space also is *mithyā*. It has *kāla-pariccheda*, time-wise limitation, because it is collapsible, as we know from the experience of sleep. Brahman, being limitless, has no spatial or time-wise limitation—means it is not born, it is not gone, it does not grow, it does not decline.

Brahman is not a particular object, and so there is no *vastu-pariccheda*, object-wise limitation. Brahman sustains time and space, and it sustains everything else that exists in time and space. No object enjoys an independent reality without the reality of Brahman. Therefore, every object is Brahman. This is the meaning of Brahman, that which is *ekam eva advitīyam*,[32] one without a second.

Let us look at the word, *advitīya*, without a second. A second thing can cause three types of *bheda*, difference, to a given thing—*sajātīya*, *vijātīya* and *svagata bheda*. A coconut tree, for instance, is different from other trees within its own species. There are many coconut trees, and this is one of them. This is *sajātīya-bheda*, a limitation caused within one's own species.

Then there is *vijātīya-bheda*. *Vijāti* means something belonging to a different species. A tree, for

---

32 *Chāndogyopaniṣad* (6.2.1).

instance, is different from the rocks, rivers, and so on. If the tree is a coconut tree, then there are varieties of trees like an areca nut tree, an oak tree, and so on that are different from the coconut tree. In the genus of coconut tree itself there is a dwarfed coconut tree, a hybrid coconut tree; there too, there are varieties. Things that come under botany, things that come under zoology, and things that come under geology are all different. Within botany itself there are varieties of plants like a vine, a creeper, a small plant, a big tree and so on. A *jāti*, species, keeps on dividing itself endlessly. But you can bring them all under one *jāti*, one subject matter of botany, because they have certain commonness about them. The coconut tree is distinct from a dog that comes under zoology. This is called *vijātīya-bheda*, a limitation caused by things of different species.

Finally, there is *svagata-bheda*, difference within a given species. A given tree has varieties of differences within itself like the leaves, the flower, the fruit, the trunk, and so on.

Taking one's own body, one can see all these *bheda*s. It has *sajātīya-bheda*, because there are many human bodies. It has *vijātīya-bheda*, because it is different from the body of any other being, like a dog and so on. Then, it has *svagata-bheda*, varieties within the body such as the head, shoulders, hands and so on, each one being different from the other.

All these *bheda*s are not there in Brahman. There is only one non-dual Brahman that is revealed by the *śāstra*. All that is here is that Brahman. Since a second Brahman is not there, there is no *sajātīya-bheda*, limitation or difference caused by the same species. Further, as there is nothing other than Brahman, there is no *vijātīya-bheda*, limitation caused by a different species. Brahman is *satya*, and everything else is *vikāra*, apparent modification, and hence *mithyā*.[33] *Mithyā* cannot be counted along with *satya*. Brahman being non-dually one, and everything else being *mithyā*, does not add to the one. In Brahman itself there are no parts and hence there is no *svagata-bheda*. Brahman is *satyaṁ jñānam anantam*. It is pure *caitanya*, consciousness, which is neither knower-known-knowledge but the truth of all the three.

Tad means *pratyagātman*, the inner self, consciousness. *Tad* is predicated here to Brahman. The subject matter *pratyagātman* has already been introduced, about which the teacher reveals something here. We do not really require a *pramāṇa* to arrive at the existence of oneself. By *dṛg-dṛśya-viveka*—subject-object analysis, we can come to know the subject, the self, is not subject to objectification. Recognising this self-revealing consciousness is Brahman, is the result of *vedānta-pramāṇa*.

---

33 *vācārambhaṇam vikāro nāmadheyam mṛttiketyeva satyam* (*Chāndogyopaniṣad* 6.1.4).

Suppose I say, '*tvam asi*, you are,' you do not get anything out of this sentence without knowing the predication. *Tvam* is the subject about which something is going to be revealed. Here, an *ākāṅkṣā*, expectancy, is created to hear what the predication is; what is it that the speaker wants to convey about the subject? Suppose, I do not say anything after saying *tvam asi*, what does it mean? Each one, according to his or her psychology, will read the silence. "You are," creates, in the listener, an expectancy. The speaker fulfils the expectancy, communicating what he or she intends to convey, which is called *vivakṣā*.[34]

The subject, *śrotrasya śrotram*, is already introduced, but needs to be predicated. This is where *pramāṇa* walks in to say, "*tad eva brahma tvaṁ viddhi*—you understand 'that' to be Brahman." That ear of the ear which is not objectified by the organ of speech, and because of which the organ of speech functions, is *advayaṁ brahma*, non-dual Brahman, and that Brahman you are. That means there is nothing other than you; the thought is not other than you, the knower is not other than you, the object of thought is not other than you. Any other knowledge implies a knower-known difference. Here, the knower is you, the knowledge is you, and the known is you. That is the revelation.

---

[34] *vaktum icchā*—the intention (*icchā*) to say (*vaktum*).

The teaching is, "May you understand that to be Brahman." There are no two entities here—yourself and Brahman. You are Brahman. If you are ignorant, well, Brahman makes that ignorance exist and known. Like anything else, this ignorance also is *mithyā*. What does not exist by itself, but draws its existence from something else is *mithyā*. Ignorance draws its existence from the same consciousness alone. Hence, ignorance is also *mithyā*; it goes away in the wake of knowledge. Therefore, *tad eva brahma tvaṁ viddhi*. Let there be no ignorance with reference to the fact of the self being consciousness, *satyaṁ brahma*. That is the whole intention of the teaching.

That *vṛtti*, the cognitive thought that takes place in one's *buddhi* as a result of teaching, is known as *akhaṇḍākāra-vṛtti*, a cognition in which the knower-known-knowledge are resolved into one awareness. That means all the three are you.

Generally, a *vṛtti* is the connecting link between the object of knowledge and the knower. When you say, "This is a pot," pot is the object and you are the knower of the pot. The *pramāṇa-phala*, the result of operating a means of knowledge, goes to you, the knower. Between you and the pot, the connecting link is *tadākāra-vṛtti*, the thought having the form of a pot. *Ākāra* means a form. A given thought assumes the form of the object it objectifies through perception, inference, words, or recollection.

You, the knower, look at the thought and say, "This is a pot." That pot thought is called *idaṁ vṛtti*. You are the knower all the time. Therefore you say, "I am the knower, and the whole world of objects is different from me." With this kind of division in thoughts, you move around knowing different things in the world.

Now, you are told by the *śāstra, tad eva brahma tvaṁ viddhi*, understand that Brahman you are. That consciousness is Brahman which is the mind of the mind, without which there is no thought, there is no object of thought, and there is no knower.

Further, on analysis, you recognise that Brahman as the intelligent and material cause of the *jagat*. That means the whole creation is non-separate from Brahman. Therefore, your body is Brahman, your senses are Brahman, your mind is Brahman, the knower is Brahman, the cognition is Brahman; everything is Brahman. In this vision you recognise the invariable consciousness *cit*, as *satyaṁ brahma*.

In other words, *cit* is *sat*. Once you say Brahman is *satya*, everything—the knower-known-knowledge—is Brahman. That means it is the whole. That is why it is called *ānanda* or *ananta*. Being the whole, it is not an object of any of these words, but rather known more by implication. You are not in any way, anywhere, circumscribed, limited.

"That consciousness is Brahman" is the *mahā-vākya*, a sentence revealing the oneness of you and Brahman.

It is not right to say that there are only four *mahā-vākyas*. This *mantra*, '*tad eva brahma tvaṁ viddhi*,' is also a *mahā-vākya*. If one accepts only four *mahā-vākyas*, then one will miss it when one studies *Kenopaniṣad* as the *upaniṣad* obtaining in one's recension. Every *upaniṣad* must have a *mahā-vākya*, not just four *upaniṣads*. For the sake of *samanvaya*, showing that all four Vedas have only one *tātparya*, vision, four *mahā-vākyas* are quoted, one from each Veda: *tat tvam asi* from Sāmaveda; *ahaṁ brahmāsmi* from Yajurveda; *prajñānaṁ brahma* from Ṛgveda, and *ayam ātmā brahma* from Atharvaveda. In fact, every *upaniṣad* has *mahā-vākyas*. Without a *mahā-vākyā* there is no *upaniṣad*, there is no *Gītā*, and there is no *śāstra* either. Any *śāstra* reveals what is to be revealed, and therefore, *mahā-vākyas* are seen in all the *upaniṣads*.

In *Chāndogya Upaniṣad*, the *mahā-vākya* '*tat tvam asi*' was repeated nine times from different standpoints. Here too, it is the same. We have a few *mantras* repeating '*tad eva brahma tvaṁ viddhi*' from different standpoints. One *mahā-vākya* is repeated many times. In *mahā-vākyas* there are no differences. It is not proper to create differences among them, like some people do. Some claim that, *tat tvam asi* is an *upadeśa-vākya*, a sentence giving the teaching; *ahaṁ brahmāsmi* is an *anubhava-vākya*, a sentence revealing the experience of oneness, and so on. The whole *upaniṣad* is meant for *upadeśa*, revealing an equation between *jīva* and Īśvara.

Hence, one cannot make differences in the *mahā-vākya*s that are meant to reveal this equation, this non-difference.

In this *mantra,* there is also a negation of what is not Brahman. Brahman is generally understood as God, the cause of the world. People worship Brahman as Viṣṇu, as Śiva. Is that not Brahman? It is Brahman as long as you include yourself. That which includes both the subject and the object is Brahman. *Nedaṁ yad idam upāsate*: Not this, which people meditate upon.

Upāsate means 'people worship'. The *śāstra* does not criticise or condemn *upāsanā;* on the contrary *upāsanā* is included. However, one should not construe that the form alone is Brahman. When a topic is considered, due respect is given to the topic. The consideration is showing respect.

Upāsanā is fine, but the *upāsya,* one whom you worship, includes you the *upāsaka* too. If the *upāsya* and the *upāsaka* are one, then the *upāsanā-phala,* the ultimate result of worship, is gained; the pay off is recognising the fact that both the *upāsaka* and the *upāsya* are sustained by one consciousness, Brahman, which is *śrotrasya śrotram*; that is why it is *satyam*. Therefore, what people worship is also Brahman, but that alone is not Brahman. These are sentences revealing an equation and one has to see the truth of these sentences. One has to inquire into them thoroughly, curbing the tendency to gloss over.

Mantra 5

यन्मनसा न मनुते येनाहुर्मनो मतम्।
तदेव ब्रह्म त्वं विद्धि नेदं यदिदमुपासते ॥ १.५ ॥

yanmanasā na manute yenāhurmano matam,
tad eva brahma tvaṁ viddhi nedaṁ yad idam upāsate. (1.5)

yat – which; *manasā* – by the mind; *na* – not; *manute* – thinks/objectifies; *yena* – by which; *āhuḥ* – they say; *manaḥ* – the mind; *matam* – is known; *tad* – that; *eva* – alone; *brahma* – Brahman; *tvam* – you; *viddhi* – know; *na* – not; *idam* – this; *yat* – which; *idam* – (as) 'this'; *upāsate* – (people) worship

May you know that alone to be Brahman, which a person does not objectify through the mind, (but) by which the mind is known, and not this that people worship as an object.

Yanmanasā na manute: That which a person does not objectify through the mind. The subject (for the verb *manute*), '*ko 'pi puruṣaḥ*, no person', has to be brought in. That means no person can know that *vastu* by the mind at any time. *Yena āhurmano matam*: That by which, they say, the mind is objectified, is pervaded.[35]

---

[35] मतं विषयीकृतं व्याप्तम्। (केनभाष्यम्)
The mind is pervaded, objectified

The word '*matam*' conveys two meanings—that because of which the mind itself is known or that because of which the mind is capable of knowing.

A sound heard, or a form seen—both are cognised in the mind alone. In every cognition there is an object involved in the form of a *vṛtti*. A sound heard is the object of that *vṛtti*, a form seen is the object of that *vṛtti*, and so too with smell, taste and so on.

Now, is consciousness an object of a *vṛtti*? No, it is not the object of a *vṛtti*. It is the content, the *svarūpa* of the *vṛtti* by which, the knowledgeable people say, the mind is known, the mind is able to do its job.[36] The presence of consciousness alone makes the mind objectify everything; but the mind itself cannot objectify consciousness.[37] That consciousness is there in every perception.

Being the invariable in every cognition consciousness is the *satya* of the knower, *satya* of the known and *satya* of the knowledge. All three are sustained by consciousness. Being all the three, it is

---

36 अन्तःस्थेन हि चैतन्यात्मज्योतिषा अवभासितस्य मनसो मनन-सामर्थ्यम्। (केनभाष्यम्)
By the light of consciousness obtaining within is the mind lighted (made conscious); that mind has the power to objectify.

37 मनसा यत् चैतन्यज्योतिः मनसोऽवभासकं न मनुते न सङ्कल्पयति नापि निश्चिनोति लोकः। (केनभाष्यम्)

The light of consciousness which lights up the mind, which, one does not objectify or know.

ananta, limitless. I, the consciousness, am that *satyaṁ jñānam anantaṁ brahma*.

Seeing this fact, one sees everything is Brahman. First, one sees what is, then everything else stands related to it very clearly. For instance, if the vision of gold is clear, then the ornaments—chain, bangle, ring, and so on—do not displace one's vision of gold. Similarly, any object of knowledge cannot displace or negate the *satya*. The names and forms keep changing but in all of them the vision of *satya* does not change.

Mantra 6

यच्चक्षुषा न पश्यति येन चक्षूꣳषि पश्यति ।
तदेव ब्रह्म त्वं विद्धि नेदं यदिदमुपासते ॥ १.६ ॥

yaccakṣuṣā na paśyati yena cakṣūṁṣi paśyati,
tad eva brahma tvaṁ viddhi nedaṁ yad idam upāsate. (1.6)

yat – which; *cakṣuṣā* – with the eye; *na* – not; *paśyati* – one sees; *yena* – by which; *cakṣūṁṣi* – the eyes; *paśyati* – see; *tad* – that; *eva* – alone; *brahma* – Brahman; *tvam* – you; *viddhi* – know; *na* – not; *idam* – this; *yat* – which; *idam* – (as) 'this'; *upāsate* – (people) worship

You know that alone to be Brahman which (one) does not see with the eyes, (but) by which one sees the (functions of the) eyes, and not this that people worship as an object.

Here, the *vastu* that was revealed as the ear of the ear and so on is now severally pointed out with reference to every sense organ, the mind, and even *prāṇa*. Pointing out the *vastu* severally is important in that the invariable nature of consciousness is intimately recognised in this method. It is one thing to say that objects are many and varied, and in the perception of these varied objects, consciousness is present invariably. But one has to dwell upon this fact, for which one has to take up every sense organ and see the invariable presence of consciousness in each of their functions.

With reference to the eyes, you see the invariable nature of consciousness being present in every visual perception. If the colour is red or white, it is red colour consciousness, white colour consciousness respectively. The sounds are many and distinct but the presence of consciousness in each perception of sound is the same. So too, with the sense of smell; in each cognition of smell the consciousness is the same. Similarly, in each varied sense of taste, consciousness is the same. In all the different forms of touch, the invariable consciousness is present.

Further, we look at all of them together. All these perceptions go to the mind. The mind has to undergo a relevant thought change, whether the perception is a sound or a form or colour and so on. In all these relevant forms of cognition you recognise the same invariable consciousness.

Even though *śāstra* can just say in one sentence—that which is not objectified by the sense organs and because of which the sense organs function is Brahman, and that Brahman you are—it takes the pain to mention each sense organ severally. This method of repetition is employed in the *upaniṣad*s to drive home a fact. The whole section becomes a theme for contemplation. Contemplation does not reveal anything new, but at the same time, it gives you clarity of the subject matter of contemplation.

Yat cakṣuṣā na paśyati: That which a person does not see with the eyes. *Yena cakṣūm̐ṣi paśyati*: That in whose presence the eyes are able to see.[38] The plural word *cakṣūm̐ṣi* has to be read as *cakṣurindriyam*.[39] The *vastu* is that in whose presence the eyes are able to see, but which the eyes cannot objectify. That *vastu*, naturally, is consciousness, because the activity

---

[38] येन चक्षूंषि अन्तःकरणवृत्ति-भेदभिन्नाः चक्षुर्वृत्तीः पश्यति चैतन्यात्मज्योतिषा विषयीकरोति व्याप्नोति। (केनभाष्यम्)

By which light of consciousness the eyes, the various thought modifications relevant to perception, see, objectify, pervade (the objects of perception).

[39] *Cakṣūm̐ṣi* should be read in the singular form as *cakṣurindriyam* because of the singular verb '*paśyati*' and the plural form of the noun *cakṣūm̐ṣi* is *chāndasa*, a Vedic expression.

of perception is involved here. That self-revealing consciousness alone is *satyaṁ brahma*. The *cit* consciousness is timeless, *sat*, which is the truth of everything. Consciousness, *pratyagātman*, is the *lakṣyārtha*, the implied meaning of the word '*tvam*'. This is equated to *tat-pada-lakṣyartha*, the implied meaning of the word '*tat*' which is *satyaṁ jñānam anantaṁ brahma*. Everything is Brahman and that Brahman is you.

Mantra 7

यच्छ्रोत्रेण न शृणोति येन श्रोत्रमिदꣳश्रुतम् ।
तदेव ब्रह्म त्वं विद्धि नेदं यदिदमुपासते ॥ १.७ ॥

yacchrotreṇa na śṛṇoti yena śrotramidaṁ̐ śrutam, tad *eva brahma tvaṁ viddhi nedaṁ yad idam upāsate. (1.7)*

yat – which; *śrotreṇa* – with the ear; *na* – not; *śṛṇoti* – one hears; *yena* – by which; *śrotram* – the ear; *idam* – this; *śrutam* – is heard; *tad* – that; *eva* – alone; *brahma* – Brahman; *tvam* – you; *viddhi* – know; *na* – not; *idam* – this; *yat* – which; *idam* – (as) 'this'; *upāsate* – (people) worship

May you know that alone to be Brahman which (one) does not hear with the ear, (but) by which this ear hears, and not this that people worship as an object.

Yat śrotreṇa na śṛṇoti: That which one does not hear by the ear. The *vastu* is not heard by the ears. It is not an object of the sense of hearing.[40] Brahman does not have any sound wave or frequency. *Yena śrotram idaṁ śrutam*: By which sound is heard, which means *yena śrotrendriyaṁ sva-kārya-kṣamaṁ bhavati*, that by which this sense of hearing is capable of its function. Sounds are heard by the ear,[41] because the ear is capable of hearing. How does it become capable? Because of something else. That something else is consciousness which is not heard by the ears, but which lends its existence for the ears to hear. The ears themselves cannot hear without consciousness and that is the *ātman*. That is to be understood as *satya*. This is how the *vicāra*, inquiry, leads you to see, to recognise the invariable *caitanya* and everything else becomes the object of that *caitanya*. This is *dṛg-dṛśya-vicāra*, seer-seen inquiry.

This inquiry has to be carried further by analysing the reality of the seen. Unless you recognise the seen

---

40 यत् श्रोत्रेण न शृणोति दिग्देवताधिष्ठितेन आकाशकार्येन मनोवृत्तिसंयुक्तेन न विषयीकरोति लोकः। (केनभाष्यम्)

That which one does not hear by the sense of hearing—born of (subtle element) space, presided over by the deity of quarters and aided by the mental *vṛttis*—does not objectify.

41 श्रुतं यत्प्रसिद्धं चैतन्यात्मज्योतिषा विषयीकृतम्। (केनभाष्यम्)

The well known ear is pervaded by the light of consciousness that is the self.

objects in terms of consciousness, understanding of *mahā-vākya* is not possible. When consciousness is seen as *kāraṇa,* cause, that is *satyaṁ brahma,* then everything else being *kārya,* effect, is seen as *mithyā.* You need not remove the *mithyā* to find the *satya.*

Suppose, I tell a person, "The wave is *mithyā,* the water is *satya;* go and see the water." Then he goes and sits on the beach waiting for all the waves to subside so that he can see the water! Does he need to wait to see the water? No. When the wave, *mithyā,* is seen, the water, *satya,* is also seen; you cannot have *mithyā* without *satya* being recognised.

Then, why do people not recognise *satya*? That is because *satya* happens to be you. The knower himself is *mithyā;* he is a knower only with reference to what he knows or does not know. Unless the knower's *satya* is understood, one is not going to understand the *satya* of the knowledge and known. The knower's *satya* is hidden. That is why one requires *śāstra.*

Therefore, when the *mantra* says, *yena śrotram idaṁ śrutam,* it means the consciousness that is present behind the *śrotṛ,* the hearer, the *śravaṇa,* the hearing and the *śabda,* the sound that is heard. The *satya* of all three is Brahman, and that Brahman is this consciousness. In this method of teaching, we include everything. Nothing is beyond *ātman,* consciousness. There is no such thing as *anātman* apart from *ātman.* If this is not understood, it causes a serious problem of dissociation, wishful denial of realities. What is negated has to be included in the *ātman*.

The inquiry begins with who you are, with reference to your perception, your knowledge. There is no other way of pointing out the *pratyagātman* being the consciousness which is the meaning of *tvam*, you. Then, that consciousness is pointed out as *satya*—that is the revelation of the *śāstra*. Therefore, *tvam tad brahma asi iti viddhi*, may you recognise yourself as that Brahman.

Nedaṁ yad idaṁ upāsate: (Brahman is) not this that people worship. The negation applies not only to an altar of worship or form of worship, but to a sound also, like *om*. People do meditation on *om*. *Om* is a *pratīka*, a sound symbol. That consciousness by which the sound *om* is heard is Brahman, the meaning of the word *om*. One should not go away with the idea that the sound *om* is Brahman.

The verb *upāsate* is plural. The people, the seekers meditate, worship, chant, etc. All these are important. But both the *upāsaka*, the meditator, and the *upāsya*, the object of meditation, are Brahman, and that Brahman is you, the *caitanya* in whose presence the ears function as ears.

Mantra 8

यत्प्राणेन न प्राणिति येन प्राणः प्रणीयते ।
तदेव ब्रह्म त्वं विद्धि नेदं यदिदमुपासते ॥ १.८ ॥

yatprāṇena na prāṇiti yena prāṇaḥ praṇīyate, tad eva brahma tvaṁ viddhi nedaṁ yad idam upāsate. (1.8)

yat – which; *prāṇena* – by *prāṇa; na* – not; *prāṇiti*– one remains alive; that is, breathes; *yena* – by which; *prāṇaḥ* – the *prāṇa; praṇīyate*– is sustained; *tad* – that; *eva* – alone; *brahma* – Brahman; *tvam* – you; *viddhi* – know; *na* – not; *idam* – this; *yat* – which; *idam* – (as) 'this'; *upāsate* – (people) worship

May you know that alone to be Brahman which is not sustained by the *prāṇa*, (but) by which the *prāṇa* is sustained, and not this that people worship as an object.

Yat prāṇena na prāṇiti: That which is not sustained by the *prāṇa*. *Yena prāṇaḥ praṇīyate*: By which this *prāṇa* is sustained. The *prāṇa* with its five-fold function sustains this body[42] and makes it alive. *Prāṇa* stands for the entire system that supplies energy for all forms of activity, including thinking.

---

42 स्वव्यापारं शरीरधारणलक्षणं करोति ।

It (*prāṇa*) does its job of sustaining the body.

The *ātman*, consciousness, is not sustained by *prāṇa*. The *ātman* of the *jīva* who indwells this body and breathes, is consciousness without which there is no *jīva*, no *prāṇa*.[43] *Tad eva brahma tvaṁ viddhi*, may you know that consciousness, the *ātman*, is Brahman.

In *prāṇa-upāsanā*, *prāṇa* is looked upon as *hiraṇyagarbha*, but that includes you, the *upāsaka*. There is no Brahman minus you. Brahman means both the *upāsaka* and the *upāsya* are included. The meditator is the knower, the meditated is the known; Brahman is both, knower and known. Therefore *nedaṁ yad idam upāsate idaṁtayā yad upāsate janāḥ*, that which people worship as 'this' is not Brahman.

When I say, what you meditate upon is not Brahman, it does not mean Brahman is not present in the object of meditation. Brahman includes you, and that is the intention. Brahman is both the knower and the known. Therefore, either you know it or you do not know it. There is no half knowledge of Brahman. We need to correct this kind of thinking. The whole Vedanta is meant to correct the wrong thinking and make thinking proper.

---

[43] येन चैतन्यात्मज्योतिषा अवभास्यत्वेन स्वविषयं प्रति प्राणः प्रणीयते । (केन भाष्यम्)
Being lighted by which light of consciousness *prāṇa* is led towards its field of function.

CHAPTER 2

Mantra 1

यदि मन्यसे सुवेदेति दहरमेवापि[44]
नूनं त्वं वेत्थ ब्रह्मणो रूपम्।
यदस्य त्वं यदस्य देवेष्वथ नु मीमाꣳस्यमेव ते।
मन्ये विदितम्॥ २.१॥

yadi manyase suvedeti daharam evāpi
nūnaṁ tvaṁ vettha brahmaṇo rūpam,
yad asya tvaṁ yad asya deveṣvatha nu mīmāṁsyam eva te, manye viditam. (2.1)

yadi – suppose; *manyase* – you think; *suveda* – I know very well; *iti* – thus; *daharam* – little; *eva* – only; *api* – then; *nūnam* – certainly; *tvam* – you; *vettha* – know; *brahmaṇah* – of Brahman; *rūpam* – nature; *yad* – which; *asya* – of this; *tvam* – you; *yad* – which; *asya* – of this; *deveṣu* – in the gods; *atha* – therefore; *nu* – definitely; *mīmāṁsyam* – to be inquired into; *eva* – only; *te* – by you; *manye* – I consider; *viditam* – known

(Teacher): If you think, "I know Brahman very well," then, you know only very little of Brahman's nature (that is expressed) in the

---

44 दभ्रमेव इति वा पाठः।

human beings and in the gods. Therefore, Brahman is still to be inquired into by you. (Disciple): I consider (Brahman) is known.

Yadi manyase suveda iti: Suppose you conclude, "I know Brahman very well." The prefix *su* gives a special meaning here, that of knowing like one knows an object. The teacher says, "If any one of you were to conclude, 'I know Brahman,' then you know very little of Brahman's nature, the truth of Brahman." It means that you do not know; because, remaining as a knower one cannot know Brahman.

Yad vettha tad daharam eva api nūnam: (Then) whatever you know about Brahman, that certainly is very little. *Yad tvam asya brahmaṇaḥ rupam iti*: Knowing the nature of Brahman as yourself along with the body, mind, and so on.

Further, *deveṣu madhye yaḥ kaścit*, taking Brahman as one among the deities like Indra, Agni and so on, or among the Gods like Viṣṇu, Śiva and so on, whom you worship. Then, certainly, you know precious little of Brahman. The word *daharam* or *dabhram* means *alpam*, very little.

It was said earlier, *nedaṁ yadidam upāsate*, Brahman is not what people worship as 'this'. People do consider their *iṣṭa-devatā*, favourite deity, as an exalted God in whom all the Gods are included, as the ultimate truth. That is correct and is, indeed, an enlightened way of looking at one's *iṣṭa-devatā*. But if one thinks that this God alone is Brahman, one is excluding oneself from that Brahman. It means one does not know Brahman at all. The *śāstra* drives home the truth that Brahman is not an object.

Anything that one says about, 'I know this is Brahman,' is also Brahman. It is like the blind men touching different parts of an elephant and each claiming that the elephant is like a wall, a pillar, and so on. All of them are talking about the elephant, but not the whole elephant. Similarly, any one thing you claim as Brahman, is Brahman, no doubt, but that is not the whole vision. Therefore, what should one do?

The teacher says, *atha nu mīmāṁsyam eva*: definitely you have to do further inquiry. *Atha nu* means therefore. It means you have to further listen to the *śāstra* and analyse it properly. *Mīmāṁsā* is analysis of the sentences of the *vedānta-śāstra* that reveal Brahman. Even though there is only one sentence that reveals the truth, everything else is meant to make the understanding of that sentence possible. Therefore, the whole *śāstra* has to be analysed.

Hearing this statement from the teacher would make the students silent. But one student said, "*manye viditam,* I consider Brahman is known (by me)." Maybe others also knew, but they did not dare to say.

When this disciple said, "Brahman is known (by me)," Brahman becomes the object of knowing. Knowing this fact the student continues, making his statement well supported by an additional sentence, to be free from any blemish.

Mantra 2

नाहं मन्ये सुवेदेति नो न वेदेति वेद च ।
यो नस्तद्वेद तद्वेद नो न वेदेति वेद च ॥ २.२ ॥

nāhaṁ manye suvedeti no na vedeti veda ca,
yo nastad veda tad veda no na vedeti veda ca. (2.2)

na – not; *aham* – I; *manye* – consider; *suveda* – I know well; *iti* – thus; *na u* – not; *na* – not; *veda* – know; *iti* – thus; *veda* – I know; *ca* – also; *yaḥ* – who; *naḥ* – among us; *tad* – that; *veda* – knows; *tad* – that; *veda* – he knows; *na u* – not; *na* – not; *veda* – knows; *iti* – thus; *veda* – knows; *ca* – also

I do not consider, "I know (Brahman) well." Nor do I not know. I know and I do not know as well. Among us, whoever understands that statement 'It is not that I do not know. I know and I do not know as well,' he knows that (Brahman).

Nāhaṁ manye suveda iti: I do not consider that I know Brahman. The disciple uses the same expression '*suveda*' used by his teacher and says, "I do not look upon Brahman as something that is an object of my knowledge." That is the idea. Brahman is not an object of knowledge. When you say, "I know the pot," then pot is an object different from you, the subject. Similarly, if you say, "I know Brahman," then Brahman becomes an object other than you, the subject. But the disciple says that he does not mean that at all. If he were to mean it that way, then definitely he would not know Brahman. By saying, '*nāhaṁ manye suveda*,' the disciple has already eliminated the possibility of Brahman being an object of perception, inference, and so on. If that is so, then how Brahman is to be known?

Brahman has the status of being known only through *śāstra-upadeśa*,[45] the teaching of the scriptures. So, the disciple tells the teacher, "*no na veda iti*: not that I do not know. You have already taught Brahman. Therefore, I cannot say I do not know Brahman. In fact, I definitely know Brahman, free from any doubt. In my understanding there is no difference between the knower, known and knowledge."

The idea conveyed here is that Brahman is not an object of knowledge, muchless is it an object of ignorance, because it is oneself. That is the meaning of the verb *veda*. Having already negated all possible

---

[45] '*śāstra-yonitvāt*' (*Brahma Sūtra* 1.1.3)

errors, the disciple has made it very clear that he knows Brahman. The word '*ca*' in '*veda ca*' meaning 'and,' is *sarva-saṁśaya-bhakṣakaḥ,* the devourer of all doubts. It stands for definiteness in terms of clear knowledge of Brahman. The statement *nāhaṁ manye suvedeti no na vedeti veda ca*, apparently paradoxical, reveals that the student knows Brahman.

Here, it is not that the disciple is someone who is unusual, and therefore got this knowledge. If so, then the uniqueness of this knowledge—being *śāstraika-gamyam,* available for knowing only from the *śāstra*—goes away. Brahman then becomes an object of some mystic experience. The teaching becomes redundant because Brahman, again, is known only as an object.

Brahman is the very content of the experiencer. An object can become an object of experience only when it is away from you by time and distance. Then it is subject to arrival and departure, whereas, Brahman is never away from you, the very nature of the subject. Since there is a means of knowledge for it, anyone can know Brahman.

So, the disciple makes a convincing statement here. *Yaḥ naḥ tad veda tad veda*: Anyone among us who understands (my) statement, knows it. If there is anyone who understands my statement—*no na vedeti veda ca,* 'it is not that I do not know. I know and I do not know as well'—well, that person also knows Brahman. It is very clear that this disciple identifies with the other disciples sitting before the teacher, and also the disciples that are going to come in later generations. He has the clarity of vision and he knows that Brahman which was pointed out as *pratyagātma-caitanya,* as *śrotrasya śrotraṁ cakṣuṣaścakṣuḥ.*

The statement 'I do not know, and I know' is not confusing for the one who knows. If one thinks it is confusing, then one does not know Brahman.

The study of the *upaniṣad* removes the ignorance of the fact that *ātman* is Brahman. Brahman is *jñeya,* to be known, not as an object of knowledge but as myself. By the words such as *yad vācānabhyuditaṁ yena vāg abhyudyate,* and so on, the *upaniṣad* points out that when you objectify Brahman, *ātman* becomes the subject and Brahman becomes the object. Therefore, Brahman should not be construed as an object.

Everybody takes the *ātman* to be the subject. There is no confusion here. Only Brahman has got to be known, because it is always taken to be an object. Therefore, it is revealed that the subject, *caitanyātman,* which is *śrotrasya śrotram,* is Brahman. Hence, the teaching is *tad eva brahma tvaṁ viddhi nedaṁ yad idam upāsate.* May you know that Brahman as neither known nor unknown, not that which people worship as an object. It is the nature of the self. Therefore, the disciple says, "Anyone among us who knows the meaning of the sentence '*no na vedeti veda ca,*' he knows." This statement will confuse anyone who does not have the *sampradāya,* the tradition of teaching. If this sentence is meaningful to one, then one knows Brahman. The meaning is clear from the context.

Mantra 3

When the conversation between the *guru* and the disciple is over, the *śruti* picks up the thread and sums up the dialogue, thereby confirming what is said in the dialogue.

यस्यामतं तस्य मतं मतं यस्य न वेद सः।
अविज्ञातं विजानतां विज्ञातमविजानताम्॥ २.३॥

yasyāmataṁ tasya mataṁ mataṁ yasya na veda saḥ, avijñātaṁ vijānatāṁ vijñātam avijānatām. (2.3)

yasya – for whom; *amatam* – not an object of knowledge; *tasya* – for him; *matam* – known; *matam* – known; *yasya* – for whom; *na* – not; *veda* – knows; *saḥ* – he; *avijñātam* – not known; *vijānatām* – for those who know; *vijñātam* – known; *avijānatām* – for those who do not know

Brahman is known to him for whom it is not an object of knowledge. He does not know (Brahman) for whom it is known (as an object).

For those who (really) know, it is not known (as an object). For those who do not know, it is known (as an object).

Mataṁ yasya na veda saḥ: The one for whom Brahman is known, he does not know. When you make a statement 'I know this object,' it means you are the *kartṛ,* the subject, who knows the *karma,* object, through a given *karaṇa,* instrument of knowing. In other words, the *vṛtti,* the thought, takes the form of the object. Any knowledge involves this duality. This is how you know an object. When you say, 'I know Brahman' then Brahman becomes an object like a pot. Therefore, one for whom Brahman is known, does not know. That is why the disciple said *nāhaṁ manye suveda,* "I do not consider that I know Brahman. Why? Because it is not an object of my thought." Then for whom is it known?

Yasya amataṁ (brahma) tasya matam: For whom it is not known, *tasya matam,* for that person Brahman is known. How it is known? It is known as the self-revealing *caitanya,* which is Brahman; so, one cannot say it is known.

The translation 'for the one who knows, it is unknown and for the one who does not know, it is known,' is a contradiction but it helps one understand that one should not look for Brahman as an object. What is, is Brahman. The subject is Brahman and the object is Brahman. If it is both the subject and the object, it is neither the subject nor the object. That means the subject and the object cannot exist apart from Brahman. This fact is said in a way that leads one to discover it.

As long the search for Brahman is there, one does not know Brahman. When the seeking stops, then also one does not know Brahman. Then when does one know Brahman? When Brahman no longer is an object of one's search, one's seeking. Giving up the search does not negate Brahman being an object of search either. One has only given up the search; but Brahman is still to be known. The concept that Brahman is *matam*, an object of knowledge, will still remain. When Brahman is no longer *matam*, a thing to be known, then it is known. That is possible only when Brahman is neither known or unknown. One for whom Brahman is no longer an object to be known, knows Brahman as himself alone. The moment you know, "I am Brahman," then the search is over. *Yasya amataṁ brahma, tasya mataṁ bhavati.*

One's whole orientation is to go about objectifying things. There are people who simply repeat the statements of *śruti* such as, "You have to know Brahman with the mind only,"[46] without unfolding them; such statements seem to strengthen this orientation. They also say, since Brahman is beyond

---

[46] *manasaivedam āptavyam* (*Kaṭhopaniṣad* 2.1.11)

the mind, it cannot be known. Hence, they say it is a matter of experience!

One does not wait for the experience of Brahman, for every experience is Brahman. In fact, *ātman*'s nature is *anubhava,* experience. The *svarūpa,* nature of every experience is consciousness, *ātman*. The *śāstra* does not talk about anything beyond one's experience at all. Nor does it talk about a special experience of Brahman. It states the truth of what we experience. Every experience is Brahman. Brahman is not what we call 'experience'. If what we mean by experience is pure consciousness, then that is acceptable.

Consciousness, the *ātman,* is Brahman and it is always there as the one in whom all experiences are strung. It pervades all experiences, sustains all experiences, and is the content of all experiences. No experience is outside pure *caitanya.* Here the *śāstra* wants you to understand very clearly that Brahman is neither the subject, nor the object, and therefore, you cannot say, "Brahman is known by me."

Vijānatām avijñātam avijānatāṁ vijñātam: For those who know, it is not known, for those who do not know, it is known. Why is it said like this? That is because the *kartṛ*, the subject, also is Brahman. The one who says, "I know Brahman," omits to include the *kartṛ* in Brahman; that is why the idea is repeated. *Avijñātaṁ vijānatām,* for those who know, Brahman is not known. So, for the wise who really know Brahman, Brahman is *avijñātam,* not an object of knowledge, because it includes the subject also. *Avijānatām,* for those who do not know, Brahman becomes *vijñātam,* known as an object.

If Brahman is not an object of knowledge, maybe, it does not exist at all. Perhaps, it is *śūnya,* zero, that is, non-existent, and has to be known as such. It is not so. There is no such thing as zero at all. Let us analyse what is zero. Is there a total zero in one's appreciation of zero? To appreciate zero, then the one who appreciates the zero must also be zero; only then is there total zero. If the one who appreciates zero is there, then there is no total zero. There is an entity there. In fact, it is a non-dual entity; there is no zero. That is why zero, in Sanskrit, is called *pūjya,* the worshipful; zero reveals that unqualified *vastu.* When one appreciates zero as *pūjya,* what is there is only one non-dual Brahman; nothing else. There is no Brahman 'plus' something else.

If Brahman is not *śūnya* but an existent reality and at the same time, it is not an object of one's knowledge, then how will one ever know this Brahman? There seems to be no way of knowing Brahman. If one takes it as an object of knowledge, then one is identified as ignorant. If one does not take it as an object of knowledge, then also one does not become wise. By simply saying, "Brahman is not an object of knowledge" one is not enlightened. One has to know Brahman. If one has to know, then Brahman should be an object. Therefore, how will one ever know this Brahman? That is a big question.

There was a time when Brahman was not known and now it is known through the teaching of the *śāstra*. Something should have happened to differentiate the two states, involving a *jñāna-kriyā*, activity of knowing. Brahman has to become an object for this *jñāna-kriyā*. If that is so, then the *śāstra* cannot say, *yasya amataṁ tasya matam*. If Brahman does not become an object of knowledge, then, what is the peculiar *jñāna-kriyā* that does not objectify Brahman? What is that special method of knowing Brahman without making it an object?

Some will say that it is not an ordinary method of knowing, wherein one's *buddhi* is used. One has to go beyond the *buddhi* to know; is it then intuition? Intuition, I suppose, can be wishful thinking—it is not taken as *pramāṇa*. Also intuiting is only with reference to what you can objectify. Here, we are talking about the one who intuits. The one who intuits is Brahman, what is intuited is Brahman, and the intuition is Brahman. This vision is totally different.

If Brahman is one of the objects in the world, then you can know it with your thought; it need not be revealed by the *śāstra*. *Śāstra* reveals that it is not available for my perception.[47] Perception as well as perceptual-data-based inference, do not have any access to Brahman. If Brahman is not recognised by any other means of knowledge, then *śruti* is the only *pramāṇa* to reveal Brahman. But *śruti* has already said, *yasya mataṁ na veda saḥ,* for whom it is an object, he does not know. How then, is it revealed by the *śruti*?

Here, one fortunate fact about Brahman is that its existence is not established by any *pramāṇa* including the *śāstra*. Anything in the world is *pramāṇa-vedya,* known through a *pramāṇa*. You know that a thing exists only through a *pramāṇa*. Heaven, for instance, has *pramāṇa-vedyatva,* the status of being known through a *pramāṇa*. The *śāstra* tells that there is a heaven. There is no means for me to disprove what the *śāstra* says. Similarly, the swami sitting here is also established by a *pramāṇa*. Anything that 'is,' has *pramāṇa-vedyatva*—either directly or indirectly one comes to know about it. Being objectified by a means of knowledge is called *pramāṇa-vedyatva*.

If the existence of anything has to be established by a *pramāṇa,* it is logical to think that there should be something already existent which does not require to be established by a *pramāṇa*. Only then can one employ a *pramāṇa* to know everything else. That one thing is *ātman*, oneself, the content of the known.

---

47 *yaccakṣuṣā na paśyati...* (*Kenopaniṣad* 1.6).

If *ātman* is Brahman here, it cannot have *vedyatva.* If the existence of the *ātman,* the self—who gathers knowledge as a knower— is also to be established by a *pramāṇa,* then who will employ the *pramāṇa,* who will get that *pramāṇa-phala*? Therefore, while everything in the world is gathered by a means of knowledge, the self does not require a means of knowledge to prove its existence. That is what we mean when we say that the self is *svataḥ siddhaḥ,* self-evident and therefore self-existent. This self-revealing *ātman,* consciousness does not have *pramāṇa-vedyatva.*

Every *pratyaya,* cognition, implies an object and the presence of this self-evident consciousness. Without consciousness there is no given cognition. There are varieties of cognitions such as space-cognition, time-cognition, sun-cognition, cloud-cognition, rain-cognition, earth-cognition, a tree-cognition, a leaf-cognition, hunger-cognition, thirst-cognition, pain-cognition and so on. One thing common in all the cognitions is the modification that takes place in the mind. A cognition means a modification in the mind. That modification is called *vṛtti* or *bodha.* Without *vṛtti* there is no cognition. Suppose you have cognition without *vṛtti,* what kind of cognition will it be? It will be cognition of everything together, because there is nothing to limit or distinguish that cognition. Since there is no need for a *vṛtti,* you will see the entire *jagat* simultaneously, or you won't see anything at all. But that is not the case. Cognitions keep varying like now a pot, now a tree, now a man, and so on. There must be a factor that distinguishes various cognitions, and that is the *vṛtti.* The presence of *vṛtti* is common in every cognition. Another common thing is the object. A cognition always pertains to an object, and therefore, there is always an object for every *vṛtti.* The object varies, but there is an object.

The third factor that is present in every *vṛtti* is the self-revealing consciousness, whether it is sound consciousness, form consciousness, or colour consciousness—consciousness is common; this is revealed as *śrotrasya śrotraṁ manaso manaḥ* and so on. This invariable consciousness—without which there is no sound, there is no colour, there is no perception, there is no inference—is said by the *śruti* to be Brahman. Brahman, the consciousness is *jñātṛ,* the knower, *jñāna,* the cognitive thought and *jñeya,* the object in the thought. All the three have their being in Brahman which is *satya.* The revelation, here, by the *śruti* is not with reference to establishing the existence of the *ātman,* like the existence of heaven, but with reference to revealing the oneness of *ātman* and Brahman, the cause of the *jagat.*

Mantra 4

प्रतिबोधविदितं मतममृतत्वं हि विन्दते।
आत्मना विन्दते वीर्यं विद्यया विन्दतेऽमृतम्॥ २.४ ॥

pratibodhaviditaṁ matam amṛtatvaṁ hi vindate, ātmanā vindate vīryaṁ vidyayā vindate'mṛtam. (2.4)

pratibodha-viditam – known through every cognition; *matam* – known; *amṛtatvam* – immortality; *hi* – indeed; *vindate* – gains; *ātmanā* – by oneself; *vindate* – gains; *vīryam* – capacity; *vidyayā* – by knowledge; *vindate* – gains; *amṛtam* – immortality

Brahman is known through every cognition. One, indeed, gains immortality (from that cognition). One gains the capacity (to know) by oneself. (Thereafter) one gains immortality by knowledge.

Pratibodha-viditam: Brahman is known through every cognition. The question, 'how to know Brahman' is answered here. *Śāstra* does not reveal the existence of an unknown Brahman. It only corrects the mistake about the self-revealing *ātman* as one subject to all limitations. Brahman is self-evident. *Śruti* tells us that Brahman is recognised right now in every cognition.

Bodha means knowledge. When you say that this is a pot, there is *bodha*, pot knowledge. Then there is book *bodha*, book knowledge, flower *bodha*, flower knowledge, and so on. In every *bodha* an unknown object becomes a known object. The factor that distinguishes the knowledge of one object from the other is the very object itself. If unknown Brahman has to become known through the *jñāna-kriyā*, then Brahman knowledge has to take place. If Brahman knowledge has to take place at a given time, then there should be an object for the word Brahman that distinguishes Brahman from all other objects. But it was said here, "Brahman is that which one does not objectify by the mind, by which the mind is known."[48] At the same time, it is recognised in every *bodha*—*bodhaṁ bodhaṁ prati*. This means that you do not require a particular *jñāna-kriyā* involving a subject-object relationship. In every form of knowledge Brahman is already manifest as *bodha*, knowledge. In the pot knowledge, chair knowledge, flower knowledge, the uncommon factor is the object, but the common factor is *bodha*, knowledge; that is Brahman. A given object cannot qualify Brahman because Brahman is manifest in and through every piece of knowledge, as its very content. It is knowledge as such, unqualified, which we say *caitanya*, consciousness.

There is no division—neither spatial, nor time-wise, nor nature-wise—between consciousness

---

[48] *yanmanasā na manute yenāhurmano matam* (*Kenopaniṣad* 1.5)

obtaining in a given form of knowledge and consciousness obtaining in another form of knowledge. It is like space, which is not divided by the various objects in space. Space remaining the same, objects come and go in space.

Consciousness always is; it does not come into existence in time. The question—"When will I come to know consciousness"—has no validity because consciousness does not go away at any time. This consciousness is the *adhiṣṭhāna,* the basis and content of any *bodha;* in this manner Brahman, *mataṁ bhavati,* is known. There is no other way of knowing Brahman.

We do accept that there was a time when one did not know Brahman, even though it is the truth of the knower and the known. But unlike an object, it is not away from you to fall within the scope of your perception one fine day. Ignorance, yes, but then, the remoteness of Brahman with the possibility of becoming an object for you to know is not there.

Bodhaṁ bodhaṁ prati pratibodham. The repetition of the word *bodham* gives the meaning 'countless *bodha*s'. You can repeat the word '*bodha*' any number of times, and what is said here is applicable to all of them. There is cognition, *bodha* throughout life.

Life is a series of cognitions. In the waking state, eyes perceive colour, ears sound, and so on; it is *bodha* all the way. When you dream, there is again *bodha.*

When you go to sleep there is no *bodha*; even 'no particular *bodha*' is also a *bodha*. That is all what life is, if you include your response the object elicits.

One has to not only deal with the objects of *bodha*, cognition, one also has to deal with *jñātṛ*, the knower. When the knower likes something, there is a liker, and when the knower does not like something then the same knower is a disliker. That *jñātṛ* also is *bodha*.

The teacher says that in every *bodha* what is invariable is Brahman. What is invariable in every *bodha* is only *bodha-svarūpa*, the consciousness. That is why it was said earlier that it is *śrotrasya śrotraṁ manaso mano yat* and so on. We do not, therefore, require a special experience to recognise Brahman. It is always in the form of *anubhava-svarūpa*, the truth of any experience.

Brahman is presented in the *śāstra* as the *satya*, cause. *Satya* is the predication and *bodha* is the *ātman* arrived at by inquiry. *Satya* never terminates, no matter what one thinks about. Think of time; it is *kṣaṇika*, momentary. Even while you think of time, a fraction of it gets terminated. Brahman being *ananta* does not get terminated—time-wise, space-wise, and object-wise.

Brahman is not an object of any thought because the thought itself is Brahman, without which thought does not exist. So, Brahman is not beyond thought.

When you say it is beyond thought, then 'beyond' is the object of thought. There is no such thing as beyond thought at all. Beyond thought is another thought, the thought of the beyond! That which obtains in every thought cannot be an object of thought. Therefore, it is *amatam*. Non-understanding of this fact is the basis for committing mistakes.

One can say that Brahman transcends thought. There is nothing wrong with that statement, provided one understands what is being said. Brahman does transcend a thought because Brahman is not a thought. That does not mean the thought is independent of Brahman. For instance, clay definitely transcends the pot when the content of the pot which is clay is understood. In the understanding of clay there is no pot; clay transcends the pot, transcends a lid, transcends a cup, and it transcends everything made of clay. Clay is not any of them and therefore it transcends all of them. It stands transcending all of them but, at the same time, the pot is not independent of its cause, the clay, and hence it does not transcend the clay. Understanding this, one can use the word 'transcend'. *Śāstra* also uses it, but meaningfully. Any experience is Brahman, whether it is in the waking, dream or deep sleep. To know that the seer, seen and the sight are Brahman, one does not require an experience, but one does require a cognitive appreciation. Any experience contains this truth and the *śāstra* is revealing it.

The dream model is very apt for assimilating this fact. In dream, the dreamer is both subject and object. But what is experienced is the difference of subject from the objects and it is real. There are desirable as well as undesirable objects, and there is also a response from you; everything is real.

On waking the dreamer discovers the dream subject was himself. The dream object also was himself. 'Himself' means not the waker because the waker was not there. It is the presence of the invariable consciousness, the self, because of whom one says, I dreamt, I am awake, I slept well. In dream, the dream-space is consciousness, the dream-time is consciousness, the dream object is consciousness; the whole dream experience—the knower-known-knowledge—is one consciousness, *jyotiḥ*. In the *Bṛhadāraṇyakopaniṣad*, there is a section called *jyotirbrāhmaṇa*. In this section, the *upaniṣad*, dealing with dream, presents the knower-known-knowledge as one *svayaṁ jyotiḥ*, light of consciousness, that is *satyaṁ brahma*. So, the dream-dreamer-dreamt is nothing but one consciousness, *satyaṁ brahma*, and it is *ananta*, limitless. Therefore, *satya* is nothing but this consciousness.

The mind that projects the dream world is endowed with tremendous power. It can project and it can cover the fact that it is a projection. In order to project it has to cover the reality, and without covering, it cannot project. If it projects without covering, it is called imagination. In imagination also there is a lot of projection, but there is no cover. Therefore, you know it is imagination; it is fun. That is the power of the mind, the power of Bhagavān, really speaking. That is how Bhagavān has given us a sample of this creative power to understand the truth of him. Otherwise one cannot relate to him at all muchless understand him. Without a model one has no referential basis to understand.

In the dream world, where does the consciousness end and the world begin? The whole world is consciousness. The object is consciousness, the subject is consciousness, all that is there is one consciousness Brahman. That is called the whole. The whole dream is 'the whole'.

Whatever is experienced at any time is the whole. If one is looking at certain microbes through a microscope, the onlooker and the microbes, together form the whole. When one looks at a thought, then the thought and the onlooker of the thought, both form the whole. Similarly, when one sees, hears, smells, tastes or touches anything, the person and the object form the whole.

The *śruti* first distinguishes the person from what he or she hears and the means of hearing by saying *śrotrasya śrotram*. Thereafter, they are seen as non-separate from *satya*; while *satya* is self-existent, self-evident consciousness. So, *pratibodha-viditaṁ matam*. One does not have to do anything special or wait for a special time, place or experience to know Brahman. Enlightenment is not an event, a happening. Nothing really happens. Whatever happens is *mithyā*. That non-happening Brahman is me, the *satya*. A non-happening Brahman allows all happenings and does not resist any happening either. *Bodhaṁ bodhaṁ prati viditaṁ bhavati,* Brahman is in and through all experiences, it is known through every cognition.

Previously the teacher said that it is not *viditam*, now he says *viditaṁ bhavati*. The student referred to this alone when he said, *manye viditam* (2.1). Here *viditam* does not mean that Brahman is known as an object of a thought. Every thought is Brahman; that is the only way to know. Brahman is known as the invariable in every thought, without termination. As *amatam* it is *matam*.

The *śāstra*, by using a couple of words like *matam* and *amatam*, reveals the whole vision. No special word has been used. *Śrotrasya śrotraṁ manaso manaḥ cakṣuṣaścakṣuḥ prāṇasya prāṇaḥ*—in all these, the words used are known to us. The known words are enough because what is to be known is the invariable in all of them. But one cannot afford to miss the extraordinary methodology employed to reveal the *vastu*.

Generally, Brahman is introduced through a cause-effect methodology. The cause is Brahman and the effect is this *jagat*. The cause is revealed to be both *nimitta*, the efficient, and *upādāna*, the material cause. Brahman, then, is not an inert material as the cause of this inert world; it is a conscious being. Once the *śāstra* presents Brahman as the *upādāna-kāraṇa*, the *jagat*, the effect, is proved to be *mithyā*.

Mithyā is a word covering one's understanding of the reality of an object. There is no object called *mithyā*. Certain things exist only in one's understanding. Beauty, for instance, does not exist anywhere else except in one's understanding, in one's appreciation. If understanding realities is philosophy, everyone is a philosopher, even taking the world as real. The word *mithyā* covers the reality of an object.

Effect is *mithyā*. If that is so, Brahman, the cause, loses its causal status to *mithyā*. From the standpoint of creation, Brahman assumes the causal status known as *īśvaratva* and everything that is created is presented in the model of five elements, gross and subtle. The *mithyā jagat*, consisting of five elements and elementals, also includes one's physical body-mind-sense complex. If all the minerals that go into the making of this complex are taken severally, then we can say, "This is calcium, not me; this is carbon, not me," and negate all of them as *anātman*. The food on the plate outside is full of fat; nothing to do with me. But once taken by me, it becomes, 'I am fat.' So, this body is part of the *jagat*. If this is understood, then it is easy to relate to the body. What makes this body alive is the *sūkṣma-śarīra*, appropriate to the given physical body. This is also a combination of things; one more reason for something to be called *mithyā*.

In any combination, no one thing is the thing. There are so many things involved in that one thing. For instance, the word 'flower' has no real substance—a single petal is not the flower, the stem is not the flower, the stamen is not the flower, the pollen is not the flower, a leaf is not the flower—but all put together we call a flower, and hence looked upon as *mithyā*. This *mithyā sūkṣma-śarīra* consisting of sense organs, organs of action, *prāṇas*, etc., is a *kārya*, an effect.

Some people take this *sūkṣma-śarīra* as the *ātman* and there are schools of thought based on this view. This *sūkṣma-śarīra* enjoying an identity as the first person 'I,' is called 'soul' by some theologies, and this soul is believed to survive death. Once the survival of the soul is accepted, then there are promises of eternal heaven or threats of eternal damnation for the surviving soul.

According to some others, the soul that carries the baggage of *puṇya* and *pāpa*, gathered in this life and in the previous lives, will go to *vaikuṇṭha* or *kailāsa* or some other world, decided by the type of baggage. Thereafter, certain *karma*s from the account of the soul combine themselves to give a new body to the soul wherein those *karma*s can be fulfilled. This cycle of birth and death goes on. Every theology, in fact, is the same with only shades of difference. All of them talk of duality—Īśvara is Īśvara, *jagat* is *jagat*, and *jīva* is *jīva*. Even though the *jagat* includes the *jīva*'s body-mind-sense complex, the *jīva* is not included in the *jagat*.

Our *śāstra* has something unique to reveal here. Brahman, the intelligent and material cause of everything, is *satya* and everything else being an effect is non-separate from its cause. So, all the effects are *mithyā*—the body is *mithyā*, the senses are *mithyā*, and the mind, in the form of thoughts, is *mithyā*. Wherever there is *mithyā*, the *satya* is present there because there is no *mithyā* without *satya*.

This makes the difference between the *śāstra* and *śūnyavāda*, the view of a school of Buddhists. The *śūnyavādins* conclude that essentially everything is zero and is therefore *mithyā* because there is no *satya*. In their view, this desk, for instance, is *mithyā* because it is dependent upon wood. Wood is also *mithyā* because it depends upon something else. That also is *mithyā* because it depends upon something else. Therefore, everything is *mithyā* because underneath there is zero. This is *śūnyavāda*.

There is no *mithyā* if there is no *satya*. Wherever there is *mithyā*, there has to be *satya*. Therefore, the table is *satya*, and the wood is *satya*, which means that *satya* is neither the table nor the wood. Then again, pulp is *satya*, an atom is *satya*, a particle is *satya*, the concept is *satya*, while *satya* is not any of them. This is how one has to understand *satya*. There is no necessity for further analysis. *Satya* is only in our understanding. There is no physical reduction here at all. Any object you cognise is *jñeya* and that is *satya* in reality.

Cognition of any object implies a *vṛtti*. That *vṛtti* also is *satya*. The *vṛtti* is not the object because an object is there without one's *vṛtti*, but, definitely, one cannot say, 'an object is' without a *vṛtti*. A *vṛtti* is always in keeping with an object that is there. Even if one does not think of objects, they are there for one to recognise. This is called *pramāṇa-prameya-vyavahāra*, operating a means of knowledge to know something. This is how the *jagat* is. For the *jagat-citra*, the painting of the world, the canvas is *satyaṁ brahma*. The *jagat-citra* is *mithyā* but *satyaṁ brahma* is present all the way.

When we say a thing is *mithyā*, it does not mean we reject it. At all levels of *mithyā*—at the level of external objects, the body, the senses, the *vṛtti* and the knower—one should not commit the error of rejecting the invariable *satyaṁ brahma* in all of them.

So *pratibodha-viditam* is *satyaṁ brahma* that is invariably present in every *bodha*, cognition. That *satyaṁ brahma* is indeed the *caitanya*, the *ātman*. Therefore, *cidātman* is understood as *sadātman*.

'I' means consciousness. When you say, 'I am', that 'am-ness' is the existence of that consciousness;

it is the nature of oneself, it is the nature of everyone, because there are not many 'consciousnesses' available. There is only one limitless consciousness, which is oneself, and which alone everybody refers to as I, I, I... Like even the pot space also is space, the room space also is space. Due to the differences in the *upādhi*, adjuncts, there are seeming differences, but essentially there is no difference whatsoever. Here, at least the space and the *upādhi*s like pot and room in space enjoy the same degree of reality. Even that kind of division is not there between Brahman and the *upādhi*s of all individuals; the *upādhi*s being *mithyā*, the division is also *mithyā*.

Next, the result of this knowledge is presented.

Amṛtatvaṁ hi vindate: One indeed gains freedom from all forms of change. The one who is no more ignorant of oneself—the self-revealing consciousness being Brahman—gains *amṛtatva*. The person being free from the notion, 'I am subject to death,' and knowing, 'I am Brahman,' gains freedom from the sense of limitation.

I am the content of a thought, and I am free from the thought itself. The conclusion, 'I am bound' is a notion but the content of that notion is not bound. It is the very content because of which the thought 'I am bound' is there. When that erroneous thought is gone, then the bondage also goes. I am free from all forms of limitation—time-wise, space-wise, object-wise.

The knowledge 'I am liberated' must necessarily be a fact that is already accomplished. If I simply say, 'I am liberated' when I feel bound, I do not gain anything. 'I am liberated' also becomes a notion imposed upon the fact 'I am bound'. If I have to be free, liberation has to be non-separate from myself, because the bondage is centred on 'I'. In knowledge, all the three—liberation, Brahman and myself—are one.

Hi means *yasmāt*, because. Because one gains freedom by this knowledge of oneself as Brahman, one gains *amṛtatva* right now and not later after death. That is why there is a spiritual pursuit.

If everything is Brahman, and if one gains freedom by recognising oneself to be Brahman, what about the various *kāraka*s, accessories, of action—the agent of the action, the object of action, the means of action, the purpose of action, etc.—that constitute the *karma-kāṇḍa*, the bulk of the Veda?

The next line answers: *ātmanā vindate vīryam,* one gains the strength by one's efforts. *Ātmanā* means *ātma-prayatnena,* by one's own efforts. Efforts imply all *kāraka*s. *Karma* covers one's prayer, one's *dharma,* one's attitudes and values, one's meditation, and so on. All these become useful. They constitute a life that is meaningful, a life that has a direction because the *puruṣārtha-niścaya,* the ultimate end, is clear. Therefore, *karma*s performed for the sake of *mokṣa* gain the status of *yoga*.

The whole life is *yoga*. We do not require living a life that is separate from what we go about but, definitely, the attitude is peculiar and separate; because everything is for the sake of *mokṣa*. That is why the *mantra* says, '*ātmanā*' in general without saying '*karmaṇā*'. Any discipline that one pursues is validated by one single word, '*ātmanā*'; one gains the eligibility or the readiness for knowledge. One is not ready now because one does not know that the solution is oneself and hence always looks for something else. One does not seem to have the required frame of mind to receive the teaching. Performing the *nitya-naimittika karma*s with the right attitude, one gains the *vīrya*, *sāmarthya*, the preparedness, to recognise the fact of oneself being Brahman.

One is not going to come across Brahman in one's spiritual journey. That knowledge will not take place automatically as soon as one gains the preparedness. One also has to make efforts to gain the knowledge.

The sentence, *ātmanā vīryaṁ vindate,* has another meaning that is closer to what is being said here. The self-knowledge takes place nowhere else except in the mind. However, the mind has to be together and tranquil. To recognise one's true self, the mind should not be looking for anything else. By that mind one gains *vīrya,* the power of knowledge which has the capacity to destroy ignorance.

What do you gain by that knowledge? *Vidyayā amṛtaṁ vindate*: One gains freedom from time-bound life by that knowledge. *Amṛta* is you. You have to know it. *Vidyayā* means by cognition, as revealed in the words: *pratibodha-viditaṁ matam*. In every *bodha*, cognition, the knower-known-knowledge is myself, which is Brahman the *satya*. It is one whole. Here, the word '*vidyayā*' in the third case does not have the sense of means employed to achieve. It is like saying by eating one appeases one's hunger. Similarly, the very gain of knowledge is indeed the gain of *amṛta*. Knowledge is the cause and *mokṣa* is the result. Since we always look for results, the *śāstra* mentions it as the end achieved.

Mantra 5

Amṛta means that which is not limited by time. Timelessness is the nature of *ātman* and one has to recognise that one is free from time. The gain is here and now. If one gains it now, one makes it. If one does not gain it now, the loss is infinite. That is being said in the following *mantra*.

इह चेदवेदीदथ सत्यमस्ति न चेदिहावेदीन्महती विनष्टिः ।
भूतेषु भूतेषु विचित्य धीराः प्रेत्यास्माल्लोकादमृता भवन्ति ॥ २.५ ॥

iha ced avedīd atha satyam asti na ced ihāvedīnmahatī vinaṣṭiḥ,
bhūteṣu bhūteṣu vicitya dhīrāḥ pretyāsmāllokād amṛtā bhavanti. (2.5)

iha – here; *cet* – if; *avedīt* – one were to know; *atha* – then; *satyam* – truth; *asti* – is; *ced* – if; *iha* – here; *na avedīt* – one were not to know; *mahatī* – great; *vinaṣṭiḥ* – loss; *bhūteṣu bhūteṣu* – in every being; *vicitya* – knowing; *dhīrāḥ* – the wise people; *pretya* – leaving; *asmāt* – from this; *lokāt* – body/world; *amṛtāḥ* – immortal; *bhavanti* – become

If one where to know here, then there is truth (in one's life). If one were not to know here, then there is great loss. Knowing this (truth) in every being, the wise people become immortal leaving from this body/world.

Now, the *śruti* tells the *phala,* result, of self-knowledge. In the previous *mantra—vidyayā amṛtaṁ vindate*—the verb *vindate* means 'one gains'. The gain is of oneself. In fact, it is the knowledge of the fact of oneself. In the gain of oneself there is no *atiśaya,* improvement, to oneself. Nothing is added to *ātman.* So this gain does not seem to be a gain at all. Here, one can raise a question "how do you call it a gain?"

The *śāstra* says, if you do not recognise it, it is a loss. There is no gain as such. Once it is a gain, then it is subject to loss because anything gained is lost in time. Therefore, the word *vindate* is commented upon here to show that it is not so much a gain, as an absence of loss. In other words, the removal of ignorance alone is the gain here. The non-recognition is a loss. When the non-recognition is a loss, the recognition, naturally, becomes a gain. This non-recognition is universal along with its offshoot, the misperception. This misperception of oneself is a heavy loss.

How much of a loss is it? The loss is of the limitless. *Na avedīt cet iha mahatī vinaṣṭiḥ*: If I were not to know, it is infinite loss. How? There are so many things I do not know; I also know so many things; there is loss, there is gain. But in self-knowledge, I do not see any gain. For instance, knowing that there is a black hole does not improve my personal lot. If I come to know about the position of Saturn in my chart, does it change its place to become favourable to me? No. Then, by knowledge of things we do not seem to gain much, and the ignorance of many things also does not seem to really cause much loss. Here, even though the subject matter of knowledge may be something big, but what is the big deal?

The teacher says—this is the absolute deal. If one were not to know in this life, there is, to say the least, *mahatī vinaṣṭiḥ*, a great loss. In fact, the gain of Brahman is the gain of the absolute, of the infinite. Naturally, not knowing that Brahman is infinite loss. You are that

Brahman and if you do not gain Brahman your loss also is infinite. You cannot say, "I do not mind." You do not want to lose whatever you hold dear. But you will definitely lose all of them, either by your departure or by the departure of all that you hold dear. When one dies, one leaves everything behind—one's house, one's bank balance, one's possessions and so on. The person had his or heart everywhere, and then had a heart attack; everything is left behind. At the time of death one leaves all these, or one may lose them even while living. But the gain of Brahman cannot be lost. If there is a gain without a loss, this is the one, only one.

The word *iha* means now, here, in this body, when the *jīva* is alive. The human body is called the *adhikāri-śarīra* because it is qualified for this *vidyā,* and thereby, *mokṣa.* Īśvara gives this human body, not by his choice, but by the *jīva*'s own *karma*. The *jīva* has earned a chance in the form of the human body. This *śarīra* is a chosen *śarīra*, the one that is the most eligible for both gathering *puṇya-pāpa,* and also, coming out of them for good. The desire for freedom from *puṇya-pāpa* is, again, not open to choice. That is the freedom that the *jīva* wants. Whether the *jīva* discerns it or not, that is exactly what it wants. This is the basic want behind all other wants.

The inner freedom centred on 'I' is sought after by every *jīva*. But when the *jīva* gets a body of a crab, it cannot grab a chance there. In the body of a crab there is no possibility of adding to one's *puṇya*. Being a crab exhausts only that particular group of *karma* for the *jīva*. But once the *jīva* gets a human *śarīra*, one has to grab it. If one does not grab it, the next form may be that of a crab! Opportunity always comes once. Somebody knocked at the door. The person inside did not answer. The knock came again, and this time the person inside asked, "Who is that?" "Opportunity," came the answer. The person inside said, "You are bluffing." "Why do you say so?" The person from inside answered, "Because you knocked twice. If you are opportunity you won't knock twice." So, if one misses this chance, please know, many kinds of other bodies are waiting to fructify! It is a loss that one cannot make up, perhaps, for ages to come. Therefore, the loss of this *upādhī* is itself a great loss, because it is meant for *mokṣa* sure.

The goal of life, to start with, is to live. Living implies being alive to realities. Then one has to know what is the reality. On questioning further, it ends up in gaining freedom from being a wanting person, *mokṣa*. Therefore, this is a *mokṣa-śarīra*, one that is meant for *mokṣa*. So, it is an opportunity lost if one does not strive for *mokṣa*. The loss is often one's conclusion, 'this is difficult to accomplish in this body, with all its limitations.' Or it can be due to a wrong philosophy that liberation is only after death. If one says that one cannot gain liberation right now, it is a great loss, for it is a loss of what is already there. As the eye of the eye, ear of the ear and mind of the mind, *ātman* reveals itself. It is in and through every cognition. One loses it only by disowning oneself, the limitless. Being the loss of the infinite, the loss is infinite Brahman.

You are Brahman. You need to know. *Buddhi* is given to you for knowing and the *buddhi* alone can know. If you do not know, the loss is yourself, the self which is Brahman. You do not want to get rid of yourself. You want to get rid of the limitations that constitute *saṁsāra*, a life of constant becoming. That is not you. If this is not recognised, one will find oneself small and insignificant, incapable of getting all that one wants. This is a life booked for *saṁsāra*. The reality is that the freedom you are seeking—freedom from time, from limitation, from *karma*—is you, the *svarūpa* of yourself.

Suppose, I know exactly what is my nature, then what do I get out of it? *Iha ced avedīt atha satyam asti*: If I were to know in this life, then there is truth in my life. Till then, it is like a dream. I go through the motions of dream living. I go after things that are not true, and try to get rid of things that I do not have to at all. The pursuit itself is false because the one who goes about doing things as 'I', as me, gets falsified. Until the dreamer wakes up, the whole problem is an imagined one and the pursuits to solve them are equally false. Similarly, when the truth of myself is missed, everything becomes as good as lost. So, if I were to know, then there is truth in anything that I do or not do in life.

The word, '*satya*' means what is gained by this knowledge is *nitya*. If one acquires a lot of *puṇya* in this life, one gets the result of *svarga*, but that is time-bound, and limited in terms of degrees of happiness. But if one were to know that this *ātman* is Brahman, then there is the result of *mokṣa*, the freedom that you are seeking in life. Thus, the result-oriented pursuit is also fulfilled here.

The word *iha cet* is significant here; it recognises the choice that one enjoys as a human being. That is why the human body is called *adhikāri-śarīra.* A bug has no choice in whether to know, 'I am Brahman'. Only a human being can be enlightened. Therefore, one has to choose. The word *mumukṣā*, meaning, a desire to be free, indicates the presence of choice. One has to deliberately choose *mokṣa*. It looks as though one also has to choose *mokṣa* like any other choice that one makes. But as one grows in one's capacity for *viveka*, discrimination, choices become less and less. *Mokṣa* becomes a choiceless choice. Mere desire for freedom is not enough; it has to be converted into a desire for knowing oneself. Then there is a possibility of knowing. Further, a possible question is answered here. I may gain Brahman, but there may be something else which also has to be gained after knowing myself as Brahman.

There is no Brahman 'plus'. Therefore, the *śruti* says, *bhūteṣu bhūteṣu vicitya dhīrāḥ pretya asmāllokād amṛtāḥ bhavanti*: The wise people become immortal after knowing the self in all the beings. The word *bhūta* has two different meanings. In this context, *bhūta* is a living being. So *bhūteṣu bhūteṣu* means in all the living beings on this earth. The living beings on the earth are grouped under four heads. They are: *udbhījja*, that which is born from the earth straight away, the entire vegetation; *aṇḍaja*, that which is born of an egg, all the reptiles, birds, and so on; *jarāyuja*, that which is born of the womb, all mammals, including all the human bodies; and *śvetaja*, that which is born of certain conducive atmospheric conditions in terms of humidity, temperature etc., microbes, micro-organisms and so on. These are the living beings.

The word *bhūta* can also be taken as the five elements—space, air, fire, water and earth. The elements account for all the elementals that are born of elements. One's own *sthūla-śarīra*, physical body, and *sūkṣma-śarīra*, subtle body, are made up of five elements, subtle and gross, and so too, the body of any living being. Therefore, *bhūteṣu bhūteṣu* means in all elements and elementals. The repetition of the word *bhūteṣu* is meant to indicate that no being or thing is left out. In all of them, *ātmānaṁ vicitya*, knowing the self.

If the self has to be recognised in another being, naturally, it cannot be confined to one's body alone. It should be one non-dual self, only then can one recognise it. Therefore, all that is there is one *ātman* alone, the *satya-caitanya*.

This is the set up. First, *satyaṁ brahma* alone was there. Then, all these elements were manifest, not separate from *brahma*. All the elementals, born of the elements, are not separate from them, and therefore, not separate from *satyaṁ brahma*. From cotton is born the yarn, from yarn is born the cloth, from cloth is born the shirt. What is the distance between the shirt and its material, cotton? There is no distance at all. Still it is cotton. If all the elements and elementals are born of Brahman, then all of them are Brahman. That Brahman is already equated with the *ātman*. Therefore, *vicitya*, knowing that Brahman as myself.

In the sentence *atha satyam asti*, what is *satya* is pointed out here. I am not the truth of this body alone, I am the truth of every body that is here, every element, every elemental, everything that is here. The individuality having its own attributes, etc., is given up in the recognition of the truth of the individual.

Asmāllokāt pretya: Giving up the notion that I am this body, etc. The *loka* here is *lokyate iti lokaḥ*, one's own experience of the body-mind-sense complex, and taking their attributes as oneself; this *abhimāna*, is called *loka*. *Pretya*, dying to this *loka*, *Ahaṁ-mama-abhimāna-*

lakṣaṇāt lokāt pretya. In other words, dying to the notion, 'I am this much alone,' one is free from bondage, *saṁsāra*. One does not travel thereafter nor one is born again. Others go to various *loka*s, fields of experience after death, and at the end of it they are again born only to die.

Knowing the truth of the non-dual self, one is liberated while living; when the body dies, there is no return because there is no individuality left any more. All that is there is Brahman who is Īśvara to everyone. All these are implied in the sentence *asmāllokāt pretya amṛtāḥ bhavanti*. Those who know this truth are called *dhīrāḥ*, wise persons. Those who are qualified to know are also called *dhīrāḥ*. So, knowing the *vastu*, *dhīra*s are not bound by time any more.

If the physical body is taken to be the *ātman*, naturally the self also is subject to death. But the self survives death and therefore is taken to be independent of the physical body. When the *jīva* recognises the truth of *ātman*, he is free from time. When the *jīva* does not recognise the truth of *ātman*, he is still around, after death, because the *jīva* is centred on consciousness. Consciousness is eternal, and the ignorance of oneself as a limited *jīva* will also continue until it is eliminated by knowledge. Death does not terminate the *jīva*. Death is only for this physical body. The *jīva* assumes a *sūkṣma-śarīra*, subtle form, at the time of death and leaves the physical body only to be born again.

It is like the dream world wherein the subtle dream body has transactions in the dream world. But, there is no birth for the one who recognises oneself as *satyaṁ brahma*.

How does one see *satya ātman* in every being, *bhūteṣu bhūteṣu*? *Bhūteṣu* is locative; does it mean *ātman* has a location? If so, I would have seen through the bodies to know the *ātman*. I would see many *ātman*s. Each *bhūta* has an *ātman*. Previously, I was counting the bodies; now I transcend the bodies and count the *ātman*s. If *ātman*s are many, one cannot become free from mortality by knowing that.

Let us first see if there is a second *ātman*. What is second? Second is a member of a set. Once you have a set of something, you have a first member, second member, third member, and so on. Otherwise you cannot count. If you count the villages in a district, there are many villages. How many taluks in a district, the number is far less, because the set is taluk. You first select a set in your mind which consists of many. In one body there are two hands. In one hand, there are five fingers. The number is one always followed by two. If there is a second thing, that means you have to count within the set.

Now, how many *ātman*s are there? To count, you must have an *ātman* set. An *ātman* set is there only when all other *ātman*s are visible. But you cannot objectify *ātman*, because it is the ear of the ear, eye of the eye, and so on. Since *ātman* is one pure *caitanya,* there is no second *ātman.* Again, there is no *ātman* set because this self-revealing consciousness is only one, and everything else is revealed to consciousness. To count a second, similar consciousness, it must exist in time and place. It has to be, therefore, a revealed consciousness, existing in time and place, and revealed to a self-revealing consciousness. A time-bound and space-bound object is an object of consciousness. Therefore, there is no second consciousness whatsoever.

Let us analyse a little more whether there is a second consciousness. Do you accept that the eyes are not the 'I'? Yes. The thought is not the 'I'? Yes. You are not the set of limbs that constitute your body. Yes. Why? Because I objectify all of them. Then you are unqualified consciousness. Yes. Between one unqualified consciousness and another unqualified consciousness no difference is possible. If there is any difference, consciousness becomes qualified.

The sense organs experience the physical world, and behind the sense organs is the consciousness. In consciousness is the group of sense organs and their perception; in sense perception alone is this perceived world, and this perceived world is non-separate from perception. A perception is non-separate from the thought, and the thought is non-separate from the unqualified consciousness. So the whole thing exists in unqualified consciousness, but gets qualified, as it were, when you see a world in front of you. Any one object that you see is consciousness 'plus' the object that you see. The flower consciousness is qualified consciousness. The chair consciousness is qualified consciousness. The sky consciousness is qualified consciousness.

Now, to see another consciousness you should remove the physical world or physical body that qualifies consciousness. The perception of the physical world goes along with the physical world. Then what is there is only one consciousness. There is no second consciousness.

This consciousness is behind all pairs of eyes, all pairs of ears and all forms of thoughts, and I am that limitless consciousness. If this is so, I cannot claim any one body, mind or set of senses as me or mine. Either all of them are 'I,' all of them are mine, or none of them is 'I,' none of them is mine. From the standpoint of 'I,' there is no body; the 'I' is free from all of them. Since all of them exist in me, all of them are me or mine. They are dependent upon me; I am independent of everything.[50] This is the nature of *satya* and *mithyā*.

The invariable self-revealing consciousness is *satya,* and everything else, drawing its reality from

---

[50] *Matsthāni sarvabhūtāni na cāhaṁ teṣvavasthitaḥ* (*Bhagavad Gītā* 9.4)

satya, is *mithyā*. *Mithyā* is not separate from *satyātman*, and so, *ātman* is non-dual. Being non-dually one[51] there is no second thing at all. What is non-dual may be taken to be more than two and, therefore, we say 'one'. One may be a set, subject to being many. So we say non-dual; there is nothing other than that exists.[52] That *satyātman* is you. Thus, *bhūteṣu bhūteṣu vicitya asmāllokāt pretya dhīrāḥ amṛtāḥ bhavanti*"seeing the above fact clearly, the wise people, giving up this notion 'I am this body,' know that they are already free.

With this, the teaching part of the *upaniṣad* is complete.

---

51 *Ekam eva advitīyam* (*Chāndogyopaniṣad* 6.2.1).

52 *Sarvaṁ khalvidaṁ brahma neha nānāsti kiñcana* (*Chāndogyopaniṣad* 3.14.1).

CHAPTER 3

What was already taught—*śrotrasya śrotram* and so on—is illustrated through an interesting story here; that is the style employed by the *śruti*.

A brief introduction

Brahman, as *jagat-kāraṇa*, cause of creation is Īśvara. This means Brahman is Īśvara manifest as *jagat*. This manifest *jagat* is viewed in a three-fold way—*adhyātma, adhibhūta* and *adhidaiva*.

A topic with reference to you, the *jīva*, who is looking at the *jagat* is *adhyātma*. You are taken into account first because you are the one who is looking at the *upaniṣad* to understand the truth of the *jagat*. *Adhi* means 'centred on'; *adhyātma* means with *ātman* as the *adhikaraṇa*, the locus, the subject matter. The self with the body-mind-sense complex is *adhyātma*.

A topic for which the locus is the *bhūta*s, the various things in the world, is called *adhibhūta*. A topic with reference to a *devatā* is called *adhidaiva*. All the three are interconnected. The *tattva*s, constituents, that are *adhyātma*, are known as *adhibhūta* when they are outside. Any fluid inside the body is indeed the water outside; *prāṇa* in the body is *vāyu*, air, outside. The temperature in the body is *agni*, fire, outside. The minerals like carbon, etc., are the earth outside.

What we smell through our nose is the molecules outside—all these are *adhibhūta.*

The *adhyātma* and *adhibhūta* are connected, just like between the sugar crystal, that is tasted, and one's taste buds, there is a connection. Even though the nose is also *adhyātma,* one does not get the taste if one puts the sugar crystal on the nose. One has to place it on the taste buds to experience the sense of taste.

This *adhyātma* and *adhibhūta* connection is by a law that is centred on a *devatā;* that law along with the *devatā* is called *adhidaiva.* For instance, when we invoke the *adhibhūta* sun as Īśvara, then Īśvara is the *adhidaiva,* the *sūrya-devatā.* Even the planets are seen as *devatās.* We can superimpose the *adhidaiva* upon the *adhibhūta.* This is like the superimposition we make when we congratulate a person who has discovered something wonderful; we pat the person's back or shake hands. Even though the brain made the discovery, the other part of his or her body, the hand, is good enough to offer congratulations.

Similarly, one can superimpose a *devatā* on the *adhyātma* and then do *upāsanā,* meditation. The eyes at the *adhyātma* level are connected to *adhibhūta,* and *adhidaiva.* The blessing of *sūrya-devatā* is necessary for the eyes to see, and also, for the light of the sun. One can look upon the eyes as a *devatā,* the ears as a *devatā,* the mind as a *devatā,* the *ahaṅkāra* as a *devatā.*

All the forms and functionaries like eyes and ears, with their expressions are Īśvara's knowledge alone. So, *adhyātma* means Īśvara in the form of the individual, *jīva*'s body-mind-sense complex. The same Īśvara in the form of the *jagat* that one experiences is *adhibhūta*. Both, the world and you, are interconnected; the world is not something different from you. Both are made up of *pañca-bhūtas*, five elements. You can gain varieties of experiences because there are varieties of means of experience, which are again connected to the *jagat*. That connection is through various laws, and Īśvara himself is in the form of these laws known as *adhiṣṭhāna-devatās*, presiding deities. If you look at the *jagat* from the standpoint of one law, then there is one *devatā*; this is how we look at *adhidevatā*.

We can say that all our inner emotions have been portrayed in the form of *adhidaiva* and *adhibhūta* in the scriptural literature. The very fact that one can analyse and understand the characters like Arjuna, Dharmaputra, Draupadī, Dhṛtarāṣṭra, Duryodhana, Śakuni and so on is because they are all there in oneself. Therefore, I can put them in the *adhibhūta* form or *adhidaiva* form because Brahman is both *adhyātma* as well as *adhidaiva*; they have continuous transactions.

The *devatās*, such as Indra, Agni, and Vāyu, are but Parameśvara in different aspects. Agni is the presiding deity of *vāk*, the organ of speech. Vāyu is the presiding deity for the sense of touch and, also, one's strength. Their existence, consciousness, and their individual powers are because of Īśvara. Existence and consciousness are common to all, but the power of each *devatā* is unique. Each sense organ is unique, having a specific area of operation, even though all of them are existent and conscious. The existence and consciousness besides their individual powers are drawn from Brahman who is manifest as individual and *jagat*.

For some people when the reality of one's eyes, ears, nose, and so on are talked about, it is philosophy and when the *devatā*s are talked about, it becomes mythology. Both are, in fact, philosophy because both reveal the truth of Brahman. Thus, we have this three-fold Parameśvara. If the eyes cannot see without Īśvara being there, the *devatā*s also cannot function without the blessings of Īśvara. *Devatā*s, like Agni and Vāyu are also like some exalted *jīva*s, having their own *upādhi*s. Even the *devatā*s can get confused if they do not know that there is *saccidānanda-ātman* Īśvara, because of whom they have the capacity to function. For instance, Agni, *svarūpataḥ*, in its intrinsic nature, is *saccidānanda brahma* and *rūpataḥ*, in its manifest form, is Īśvara. It is Īśvara who is behind all the powers that Agni enjoys. If Agni boasts, "I am Agni, and I can burn down anything on the earth," then Agni has an unenlightened ego.

An unenlightened ego is a loaded ego; it has to be lightened first, in order to be enlightened later. To be lightened, the ego has to get a blow. It does not take much time. In fact, all the prayers are meant to keep the ego light; only then does one discover one's true self. Therefore, first, one has to recognise the *rūpa* that is Īśvara, before one recognises one's *svarūpa*.

The questions *kena iṣitaṁ patati*, and *kena preṣitaṁ patati* are both answered in the *śāstra*. The answer to the first question is the common presence that is *saccidātman*, the *svarūpa*, that makes the eyes as eyes, the ears as ears, and so on; that is, it makes them function without any kind of will or motive. The answer to the second question is the distinct presence that is Īśvara who is the *rūpa*, the *karmādhyakṣaḥ*. We have to recognise both the common presence and the distinctive presence in all the functions.

Here, we have a very interesting story illustrating the distinctive presence that is Īśvara in all the functions, at the level of *adhyātma* and *adhidaiva*. This story is also meant to praise the *brahma-vidyā*. We come to know that even *devatā*s like Indra had a *guru* and were taught this *brahma-vidyā*. All these *devatā*s are highly worshipped. All the *vaidika*s invoke them and these *devatā*s get oblations from them all the time. But it is Īśvara who gives each of them the status of being an exalted *devatā*. Hence, whatever *vibhūti*, glory, they have belongs to Īśvara. But the *devatā*s, who once revelled in their victory over *ausras*, did not know that. Due to *avidyā*, ignorance, they appropriated that victory to themselves. Hence, to remove this *avidyā*, they had to be taught the *brahma-vidyā*. Having gained this knowledge they excelled over other *devatās* and thereby *Brahma-vidyā* is also glorified.

Mantra 1

ब्रह्म ह देवेभ्यो विजिग्ये । तस्य ह ब्रह्मणो विजये देवा अमहीयन्त ॥ ३.१ ॥

brahma ha devebhyo vijigye, tasya ha brahmaṇo vijaye devā amahīyanta. (3.1)

brahma – Brahman (as Īśvara); *ha* – once; *devebhyaḥ* – for the *devas*; *vijigye* – won; *tasya brahmaṇaḥ* – of that Brahman; *ha* – indeed; *vijaye* – in the victory; *devāḥ* – *devas*; *amahīyanta* – were glorified

Brahman won a victory for the *devas* (over the *asuras*). In the victory of that Brahman, the *devas* were glorified.

There was a war between the *devas* and *asuras* for the control of heaven. The good always wins. The *asuras*, who are immensely powerful and inimical to the peace and harmony in the society, have to be defeated. In this war the *devatās* won because of Īśvara's grace. Brahman—by giving *sattā-sphūrti*, and delegating all the necessary powers—accomplished the victory for the *deva*s. So, Brahman as Īśvara alone is presented here.

The *deva*s won and got all the honours, but behind that victory was the invisible Parameśvara, who is *śrotrasya śrotram*, etc. Because Parameśvara was not visible, the *deva*s were propitiated. *Amahīyanta* means they all became highly worshipped. It is not easy to defeat the *asura*s, and since the *deva*s won the war, they received the encomia.

Mantra 2

त ऐक्षन्त। अस्माकमेवायं विजयोऽस्माकमेवायं महिमेति। तद्धैषां विजज्ञौ। तेभ्यो ह प्रादुर्बभूव। तन्न व्यजानत किमिदं यक्षमिति॥ ३.२॥

ta aikṣanta, asmākam evāyaṁ vijayo'smākam evāyaṁ mahimeti, taddhaiṣāṁ vijajñau, tebhyo ha prādurbabhūva, tanna vyajānata kim idaṁ yakṣam iti. (3.2)

te – they; *aikṣanta* – thought; *asmākam* – our; *eva* – only; *ayam* – this; *vijayaḥ* – victory; *asmākam* – our; *eva* – only; *ayam* – this; *mahimā*– glory; *iti* – thus; *tad* – that Brahman; *ha* – indeed; *eṣām* – of these *devas*; *vijajñau* – knew; *tebhyaḥ* – for their sake; *ha* – as the story goes; *prādurbabhūva* – manifested; *tat* – that; *na* - not;

> *vyajānata* – they did not know; *kim* – what (is); *idam*– this; *yakṣam* – celestial form; *iti*– thus
>
> They thought, "This victory is ours only. This glory is ours only." That Brahman knew (the vanity) of these *deva*s. For their sake, Brahman manifested (in front of them in the form of a *yakṣa*). They did not recognise that celestial form.

Te aikṣanta, they, the applauded *deva*s, were under the notion that they were solely responsible for their victory. So, they thought, "This victory and glory belong to us and only to us." The word, '*eva*' shows that they negated the role of anyone else in their victory. They failed to recognise the one who is behind the body-mind-senses and who makes them function. Thus, the *deva*s were gloating in this conceit: "We won and it is our glory. We deserve this worship."

Thanks to their prayers earned before, Īśvara decided to save them. *Taddhaiṣāṁ vijajñau*: That Brahman knew their thinking. *Tat* means that (Brahman) as Īśvara who accomplished this victory because every *karma-phala* comes from him alone. The *devas* should have taken it as Īśvara's *prasāda,* but they did not. On the contrary their vanity made them take this victory and glory as theirs. That Brahman—who is *sarvajña*, omniscient, *antaryāmin*, abiding within everyone, and who is *śrotrasya śrotraṁ manaso manaḥ*—indeed, *vijajñau*, understood, this false notion of the *deva*s.

Ha is in the sense of, 'as the story goes'. In order to bless them by correcting their thinking, Brahman, assuming a celestial form, manifested in front of them. Assuming a special form for a specific purpose on the part of Īśvara is called *avatāra,* divine incarnation. Here, the celestial form of *yakṣa* is also one *avatāra.*

The *deva*s, who were celebrating their victory, did not know what was this celestial form that suddenly appeared before them. They saw the form, but did not have the *viśeṣa-jñāna,* the knowledge of the identity of the form. *Yakṣa* means *pūjya,* a form that is very arresting, fascinating, and effulgent, commanding reverence. The *deva*s, themselves being celestials, have seen all types of forms, but not this one. That they could not know this form that appeared like lightning, was itself a humbling blow to them. They might have thought, "How can anybody be around us without our knowledge?" The *yakṣa*'s presence intrigued the *deva*s.

The *yakṣa* is *prasiddha,* right in front of them, but still, there is ignorance about it. The *deva*s have *sāmānya-jñāna,* general knowledge, that this is a *yakṣa,* but not the *viśeṣa-jñāna* of his background and *svarūpa.*

Now they have the *jijñāsā,* desire to know. Because the *yakṣa*'s form is so compelling, they cannot but desire to know. Once one knows one is ignorant of something significant, one wants to know.

Mantra 3

तेऽग्निमब्रुवञ्जातवेद एतद्विजानीहि किमिदं यक्षमिति ।
तथेति ॥ ३.३ ॥

te'gnim abruvañjātaveda etad vijānīhi kim etad yakṣam iti. tatheti (3.3)

te – they; *agnim* – to the deity, Agni; *abruvan*– told; *jātaveda* – O Agni! *etat* – this; *vijānīhi* – know / find out; *kim* – what; *etat* – this; *yakṣam*– celestial being; *iti* – thus; *tathā* – let it be so; *iti* – thus

The *deva*s said to Agni, "O Jātaveda! Please find out what this *yakṣa* is." Agni replied, "Let it be so."

We learn from the word '*te*, they' that there was at least one more *deva* with them when Indra and Vāyu addressed Agni. They addressed Agni as *jātaveda*[53]—the one because of whose grace one gains all forms of wealth. Agni is the one who is invoked in all Vedic rituals, meant for different ends. O Agni! "Find out what is this *yakṣa*, from which world has it come, what is its nature."

Agni is of the nature of brilliance which lights up all dark areas. Here, it is a situation wherein there is darkness, ignorance, about the identity of the *yakṣa*.

---

53 *jātaṁ te vedaṁ dhanaṁ yasmāt iti jātavedāḥ.* (*Halāyudhakośaḥ*)

So they approached Agni first. Agni thought, after all this is not a big venture, but just a simple job of finding out who the *yakṣa* is, and said, "Okay, *tathā (astu)*– so it be."

Mantra 4

तदभ्यद्रवत्तमभ्यवदत्कोऽसीत्यग्निर्वा अहमस्मीत्य-
ब्रवीज्जातवेदा वा अहमस्मीति ॥ ३.४ ॥

tad abhyadravat tam abhyavadat ko'sītyagnirvā
aham asmītyabravījjātavedā vā aham asmīti. (3.4)

tat – (near) that; *abhyadravat* – (Agni) approached; *tam* –to that (Agni); *abhyavadat* – (*yakṣa*) talked; *kaḥ* – who; *asi* – are you; *iti* - thus; *agniḥ* – Agni; *vai* – well-known; *aham* – I; *asmi* – am; *iti* - thus; *abravīt* – told; *jātavedāḥ*– Jātavedā; *vai*– indeed; *aham* – I; *asmi* – am; *iti*– thus

Agni approached that (*yakṣa*). (The *yakṣa*) asked him, "Who are you?" (Agni) answered, "I am the well-known Agni. I am well known as Jātavedā, the bestower of wealth."

Agni went very near the *yakṣa* but still could not understand who the *yakṣa* was. Agni is *vāg-devatā*, the presiding deity for speech. The *Taittirīya Upaniṣad* says,[54] 'Words go very near Brahman but,

---

[54] *Yato vāco nivartante aprāpya manasā saha* (*Taittirīyopaniṣad* 2.4.1)

not obtaining Brahman, not being able to express Brahman, they all come back.' Thus, Agni, who lights up everything, went very near the *yakṣa* in order to ask. But before Agni could speak, the *yakṣa* asked, "Who are you?"

Everybody knows Agni. So the question, '*ko 'si*, who are you,' is a slight to Agni. It is something like asking the sun, 'Who are you'? This is the first blow to his ego. But, charmed by the fascinating form and sweet voice, Agni recovers himself and tries to be proud while answering, "Don't you know me? I am Agni,[55] I am the *ādhibhautika-agni*, I am the first deity to receive oblations in all rituals. I am also the *ādhyātmika-agni*, the digestive fire in the body. In anything that is born, I am there as temperature.[56] Without me nobody lives. Also I am known as Jātavedā, because of whom everyone gets the *karma-phala*s. I make people wealthy." The utterance of the second name, Jātavedā, is to show the pride. Agni should not have answered, if he felt so proud, but he answered under the spell of the *yakṣa*.

The *yakṣa* further asks:

---

[55] *Aṅgati ūrdhvaṁ gacchati iti agniḥ*, that which goes up always is Agni.

[56] *Jāte, jāte vidyate iti jātavedāḥ*, that which obtains in every being that is born.

Mantra 5

तस्मिꣳस्त्वयि किं वीर्यमिति । अपीदꣳसर्वं दहेयं यदिदं पृथिव्यामिति ॥ ३.५॥

tasmiṁstvayi kiṁ vīryam iti, apīdaṁ sarvaṁ daheyaṁ yad idaṁ pṛthivyām iti. (3.5)

tasmin tvayi – in you of such (greatness); *kim*– what; *vīryam* – strength; *iti* – thus; *api* – suppose; *idam* – this; *sarvam* – all; *daheyam* – I will burn down; *yat* – whatever; *idam* – this; *pṛthivyām* – on the earth; *iti* – thus

The *yakṣa* asked, "What is the power in you of such (greatness)?" (Agni answered), "I can burn down all that is there on this earth."

"Oh! You seem to be great and a popular *devatā*. To be so, you must have some extraordinary strength. What is that special strength you have?" – thus asked the *yakṣa*.

Agni replied, "I can burn anything that is on the earth, whether wet or dry." The indeclinable word '*api*' here means, 'if there is an occasion for that,'[57] if there is a necessity for burning anything. The word *pṛthivī* can be taken as the place where Agni is standing, or everything that is on the earth. It can include all other *loka*s also. Agni is everywhere, and so it can burn anything that is combustible.

---

[57] *sambhāvanāyām apiśabdaḥ.*

Mantra 6

तस्मै तृणं निदधावेतद्दहेति। तदुपप्रेयाय सर्वजवेन। तन्न शशाक दग्धुम्। स तत एव निववृते। नैतदशकं विज्ञातुं यदेतद्यक्षमिति ॥ ३.६ ॥

tasmai tṛṇaṁ nidadhāvetad daheti, tad upapreyāya sarvajavena, tanna śaśāka dagdhum, sa tata eva nivavṛte, naitad aśakaṁ vijñātuṁ yad etad yakṣam iti. (3.6)

tasmai – for him; *tṛṇam* – a blade of grass; *nidadhau* – placed; *etat* – this; *daha* – burn; *iti* – thus; *tat* – that; *upapreyāya* – Agni approached; *sarvajavena* – with all (his) force; *tat* – that; *na*– not; *śaśāka* – was able; *dagdhum* – to burn; *saḥ* – he; *tataḥ* – from there; *eva* – itself; *nivavṛte*– retreated; *na* – not; *etat* – this; *aśakam*– was able to; *vijñātum* – to find out; *yat* – what; *etat* – this; *yakṣam* – celestial being; *iti* – thus

The *yakṣa* placed a blade of grass in front of Agni and said, "Burn this (blade of grass)." Agni approached that (blade of grass) with all his force. (But he) could not burn that (blade of grass). (Then,) Agni retreated from there and said to the *devas*, "I could not find out what this *yakṣa* is."

The *yakṣa* picked up a small, dry blade of grass and placed it in front of the boastful Agni and asked him to burn it. To ask Agni to do the job of burning is itself a big insult. It would befit Agni if the *yakṣa* asked him to burn a forest. But asking him to burn just a blade of grass, that too, a dry blade of grass, is something like asking Mike Tyson[58] to fight with a five-year old urchin! That is an insult by itself. In the normal course, Agni should have brushed it aside but instead he found himself obeying the *yakṣa*. Agni himself did not know exactly why he was drawn to oblige.

Agni casually approached the blade of grass, thinking that it would burn with his approach. But the blade of grass did not burn—it remained there as it was. Agni, then, made an attempt. Nothing happened. Blazing with anger, he attacked the grass with all his force to burn it. The grass would not just burn. Agni attacked with his many tongues of flame—blue, red and so on. Nothing happened. Then he thought, 'Let me bake it,' and sat on it, then got up after giving it enough time, only to find to his dismay that the piece of grass did not even change in its colour.

Agni knew that he was up against someone who was not ordinary; he went back to the *deva*s. He told them, without narrating his humiliating experience, "It was not possible for me to find out who the *yakṣa* was."

---

[58] Name of the boxer who held the heavy-weight world champion boxing title at the time of these discussions.

Mantra 7

अथ वायुमब्रुवन्। वायवेतद्विजानीहि किमेतद्यक्षमिति।
तथेति ॥ ३.७ ॥

atha vāyum abruvan, vayavetad vijānīhi kim etad yakṣam iti, tatheti. (3.7)

atha – then; *vāyum* – to the deity Vāyu; *abruvan*– told; *vayo* – O Vāyu! *etat* – this; *vijānīhi* – know; *kim* – what; *etat* – this; *yakṣam*– celestial being; *iti* – thus; *tathā* – let it be so; *iti* – thus

Then, the *deva*s said to Vāyu, "O Vāyu, Please find out what this *yakṣa* is." Vāyu replied, "Let it be so."

Then came the turn of Vāyu, the deity of air. The other *devatā*s asked Vāyu to find out the *svarūpa*, identity, of the *yakṣa*. Vāyu is subtler than Agni. Agni has a form, but Vāyu does not, and so he can move anywhere. Therefore, Vāyu thought he could do the job. He is the one who sustains everybody, who provides life to every living organism.

He accepted the assignment. Even though it is a very simple task, he must have entertained some doubts because Agni failed. Nevertheless, he felt he could accomplish this job. He said, "I will go and find out who the *yakṣa* is."

Mantra 8

तदभ्यद्रवत्तमभ्यवदत्कोऽसीति । वायुर्वा
अहमस्मीत्य-ब्रवीन्मातरिश्वा वा अहमस्मीति ॥३.८॥

tad abhyadravat tam abhyavadat ko'sīti, vāyurvā aham asmītyabravīnmātariśvā vā aham asmīti. (3.8)

tat – (near) that; *abhyadravat* – (Vāyu) approached; *tam* – to that (Vāyu); *abhyavadat*– (*yakṣa*) talked; *kaḥ* – who; *asi* – are you; *iti* - thus; *vāyuḥ*– Vāyu; *vai* – indeed; *aham* – I; *asmi*– am; *iti* – thus; *abravīt* – told; *mātariśvā* – Mātariśvā; *vai* – indeed; *aham* – I; *asmi* – am; *iti* - thus

Vāyu approached that (*yakṣa*). (The *yakṣa*) asked him, "Who are you?" (Vāyu) answered, "I am the well-known Vāyu. I am well known as Mātariśvā, the one who freely moves in the sky."

Vāyu approached the *yakṣa* to find out who it was. The *yakṣa* was still unknown; he did not conform to anything so far known. The *yakṣa* was not available for a definition for one to categorically arrive at, or bring under any *jāti*, group, any *vyakti*, individual entity, for the *yakṣa* could not be classed as a *gandharva*, *deva*, *kinnara*, *manuṣya*, an animal, and so on. The *viśeṣa-jñāna*, particular knowledge, about the *yakṣa* was not there.

As Vāyu was looking at this *yakṣa,* and about to ask, "Who are you?" the *yakṣa* asked him in a compelling voice, "Who are you?" Vāyu might have thought of retorting back, "What a question you are asking. Are you breathing or not?" But restraining himself he answered, "I am the famous Vāyu. I am the one who makes everybody live. Any living being has to depend upon me. I do not remain in one place. I keep moving,[59] blessing everybody. I am the God of strength." The word '*aham*' in the *mantra* reveals Vāyu's pride. Further, he says, "I am known as Mātariśvā.[60] I am such a great person that I go to places where nobody else can enter." Then the *yakṣa* asked the same question.

Mantra 9

तस्मिꣳस्त्वयि किं वीर्यमित्यपीदꣳसर्वमाददीय यदिदं पृथिव्यामिति ॥ ३ ॥९ ॥

tasmiṁstvayi kiṁ vīryam iti api idaṁ sarvam ādadīya yad idaṁ pṛthivyām iti (3.9)

tasmin tvayi – in you of such (greatness); *kim*– what; *vīryam* – strength; *iti* – thus; *api* – suppose; *idam* – this; *sarvam* – all; *ādadīya* – I

59 *vāti gacchati iti vāyuḥ.*

60 *mātari ākāśe śvayati gacchati iti* - the one who moves freely in space without any hindrance.

can lift; *yat* – whatever; *idam* – this; *pṛthivyām*– on the earth; *iti* - thus

The *yakṣa* asked, "What is the strength in you of such (greatness)?" (Vāyu answered) "I can lift all this which is upon the earth."

In Vāyu's answer, the word, '*api*' means, as before, 'if there is an occasion for that, for lifting anything then.' "With my own strength, I can lift anything, take anything that is here on the earth, and get it into space." *Vāyu* is also the god of strength. He has different forms like a hurricane, a whirlwind, and so on. When he replied thus, the *yakṣa* responded as before.

Mantra 10

तस्मै तृणं निदधावेतदादत्स्वेति। तदुपप्रेयाय सर्वजवेन। तन्न शशाकादातुम्। स तत एव निववृते। नैतदशकं विज्ञातुं यदेतद्यक्षमिति॥ ३.१०॥

tasmai tṛṇaṁ nidadhavetad ādatsveti, tad upapreyāya sarvajavena, tanna śaśākādātum, sa tata eva nivavṛte, naitad aśakaṁ vijñātuṁ yadetad yakṣam iti. (3.10)

tasmai – for him; *tṛṇam* – a blade of grass; *nidadhau* – placed; *etat* – this; *ādatsva* – lift; *iti*- thus; *tat* – that; *upapreyāya* – Vāyu approached; *sarvajavena* – with all force; *tat* – that; *na* – not;

> *śaśāka* – was able to; *ādātum* – to lift; *saḥ* – he; *tataḥ* – from there; *eva* – itself; *nivavṛte* – retreated; *na* – not; *etat* – this; *aśakam* – was able to; *vijñātum* – to find out; *yat* – what; *etat*– this; *yakṣam* – celestial being; *iti* – thus
>
> The *yakṣa* placed the same blade of grass in front of Vāyu and said, "Lift this (blade of grass)." Vāyu approached that (blade of grass) with all his force. (But he) could not lift that (blade of grass). (Then,) Vāyu retreated from there and said to the *deva*s, "I could not find out what this *yakṣa* is."

The *yakṣa* had the same small dry blade of grass that was placed in front of Agni. He asked Vāyu to lift that. This was too small a job for him and he need not have attempted at all, but he did; that was the spell of the *yakṣa*. He approached the piece of grass thinking that it would fly but it did not even stir. Then Vāyu attacked it from all sides with his different forms. Even to say that Vāyu attacked a blade of grass is silly. But then, he did. He was not able to even shake it. Whatever happened to Agni, also happened to Vāyu. Vāyu, then, made a retreat with his head down, and went back to the *deva*s. When he went there, of course, he stood up nicely and said that it was not possible to know what this *yakṣa* was. He also did not narrate what happened, but Agni knew what Vāyu had faced. Both of them probably looked at each other with understanding!

Mantra 11

अथेन्द्रमब्रुवन्मघवन्नेतद्विजानीहि किमेतद्यक्षमिति ।
तथेति । तदभ्यद्रवत्तस्मात्तिरोदधे ॥ ३.११ ॥

atha indram abruvan maghavannetad vijānīhi kim etad yakṣam iti, tatheti, tad abhyadravat tasmāt tirodadhe. (3.11)

atha - then; *indram* – to Indra; *abruvan* – they said; *maghavan* – O Indra! *etad* – this; *vijānīhi*– know; *kim* – what; *etad* – this; *yakṣam* – celestial being; *iti* – thus; *tathā* – let it be so; *iti* – thus; *tat* – that; *abhyadravat* – (he) approached; *tasmāt* – from him; *tirodadhe* – (the *yakṣa*) disappeared

Then, the *deva*s said to Indra, "O Indra, please find out what this *yakṣa* is." "Let it be so," (Indra replied). Indra (then) approached that (*yakṣa*). The *yakṣa* disappeared from him (from that place).

After Vāyu and Agni returned without knowing anything about the *yakṣa*, the other *deva*s pleaded with Indra to go and find out about the *yakṣa*. Indra, the chief of all the *deva*s, was addressed as *maghavan*, meaning, the one who deserves worship. He had defeated all the *asura*s. He is the presiding deity of the hands, and their strength. Indra, thinking that he would succeed, confidently approached the *yakṣa*. As he went near the *yakṣa*, it just vanished. Agni and Vāyu did fare because they talked to the *yakṣa,* but Indra could not even get to see this being closely. This is like that person whom you want to talk to but slams the door right on your face, upon seeing you. Similarly, even though Indra stood there, but the *yakṣa* just disappeared.

Indra did not feel humiliated; his pride that 'I am Indra' was gone. He became humble.

Mantra 12

स तस्मिन्नेवाकाशे स्त्रियमाजगाम बहुशोभ-
मानामुमाꣳहैमवतीम्। ताꣳहोवाच किमेतद्यक्षमिति
॥ ३.१२ ॥

sa tasminnevākāśe striyam ājagāma bahuśobhamānām umām̐ haimavatīm, tam̐ hovāca kim etad yakṣam iti. (3.12)

saḥ – he (Indra); *tasmin* – (remained) there; *eva* – only; *ākāśe* – in the place; *striyam* – a woman (who appeared there); *ājagāma* – he approached; *bahu-śobhamānām* – (who was) very effulgent; *umām* – Umā; *haimavatīm* – daughter of Himavān; *tām* – her; *ha* – indeed; *uvāca* – (he) said; *kim* – who; *etat* – this; *yakṣam* – celestial being; *iti* – thus

Indra (remained) in that very same place. He approached a woman (who appeared there)

who was Umā, the daughter of Himavān and who was very effulgent. Indra indeed asked her, "What is this *yakṣa*?"

We need to bring in a few words to make the sentence complete, even though the meaning is obvious. *Saḥ tasmin eva ākāśe* (*sthitavān*): He remained there. 'He' refers to Indra. Indra who was humbled completely, and whose pride was gone, did not leave but stood there at the same place with devotion and surrender, which are the pre-requisites for gaining the knowledge of Brahman.

In the very same place where the *yakṣa* was standing, a *strī*, a woman appeared. Indra (with folded hands) went near her. She was *bahu-śobhamānā*, brilliantly effulgent. She was indeed Umā, who is *brahma-vidyā* in this context. Brahman is not to reveal itself any more than what it is already doing. Only *brahma-vidyā* can reveal Brahman. Therefore *śruti*, the very knowledge, stood there in the form of a woman. She was *haimavatī*, the daughter of Himavān. Or, *haimavatī* means the one who is effulgent like gold, *hema* meaning gold. Having approached her, Indra prayed to her, "Please tell me who was this *yakṣa*; what is the *svarūpa* of this *yakṣa*." Umā, who is the manifestation of *brahma-vidyā*, reveals the identity of the *yakṣa* in the next *mantra*.

CHAPTER 4

Mantra 1

सा ब्रह्मेति होवाच। ब्रह्मणो वा एतद्विजये
महीयध्वमिति। ततो हैव विदाञ्चकार ब्रह्मेति ॥ ४.१ ॥

sā brahmeti hovāca, brahmano vā etad vijaye mahīyadhvam iti, tato ha eva vidāñcakāra brahmeti. (4.1)

sā – she; *brahma* – Brahman; *iti* – as; *ha* – indeed; *uvāca* – said; *brahmaṇaḥ* – of Brahman; *vai* – indeed; *etat* – in this manner; *vijaye* – in the victory; *mahīyadhvam* – you all are honoured; *iti* – thus; *tataḥ* – from that (teaching); *ha* – indeed; *eva* – only; *vidāñcakāra* – (Indra) knew; *brahma* – (the *yakṣa* to be) Brahman; *iti* – thus

She (Umā) revealed (to Indra) that (the *yakṣa* is none other than) Brahman and said, "You are honoured, in this manner indeed, in the victory of Brahman only." From that (teaching of Umā) alone Indra knew the *yakṣa* to be Brahman.

Sā brahmeti ha uvāca: She said it was Brahman. Being asked by Indra, Umā, in the form of *brahma-vidyā*, said that the *yakṣa* was none other than Brahman. Umā further said, *brahmaṇo vai etad vijaye mahīyadhvam iti.*

The word *etad* is an adverb—all your valour, glories, the honours and praises showered on you for this victory, in the fight between *deva*s and *asura*s, is because of that Brahman alone. Brahman as Īśvara provides you with all the power to fight, and Brahman as the *vastu, saccidānanda-ātman*, provides existence, consciousness and the abilities to the senses and the mind, making them what they are. Any glory is of Brahman both in terms of existence, consciousness, and in manifest form. That means, you are not there at all; only Īśvara is. Therefore, *jiva* and Īśvara are one and the same.

The original question, *keneṣitaṁ patati preṣitaṁ manaḥ*, is with reference to the *adhyātma*, while Indra's question here is with reference to the *adhidaiva*.

The *yakṣa* that appeared is only for *upāsanā*, meditation. The one whom people objectify and worship is not really the *svarūpa* of *yakṣa*. Because of whom one is able to perform all functions, that is the *yakṣa*. That *yakṣa* is not to be gained as an object, in the form in which he appeared. He disappeared because Indra wanted to know the *yakṣa* as an object. That is why it was said earlier, *yasyāmataṁ tasya mataṁ mataṁ yasya na veda saḥ*—for whom (Brahman) is not known, for him, it is known; for whom it is known, he does not know. For whom Brahman 'is'—but not as an object—that person alone is no more ignorant of Brahman. *Śruti* is the means of knowing.

Vāyu and Agni attempted to know but they could not understand. Even Indra's attempt was futile; he also could not know the *yakṣa*'s *svarūpa*. With the help of the *śruti* alone, Indra understood, "It is Brahman, because of whom Vāyu is Vāyu, Agni is Agni and so on."

Tataḥ eva vidāñcakāra: From the teaching of Umā alone, Indra understood the *yakṣa* to be a manifestation of Brahman, which is the very self. Indra did not come to know on his own. This is the same with everybody else too.

Mantra 2

तस्माद्वा एते देवा अतितरामिवान्यान्देवान् यदग्निर्वायुरिन्द्रः ।
ते ह्येनन्नेदिष्ठं पस्पृशुः । ते ह्येनत्प्रथमो विदाञ्चकार
ब्रह्मेति ।। ४.२ ।।

tasmādvā ete devā atitarām ivānyān devān yad agnirvāyurindraḥ, te hyenannediṣṭhaṁ paspṛśuḥ, te hyenat prathamo vidāñcakāra brahmeti. (4.2)

tasmāt – therefore; *vai* – indeed; *ete* – these; *devāḥ* – *devas*; *atitarām* – excel; *iva* – definitely; *anyān* – others; *devān* – *devas*; *yat* – that; *agniḥ* – Agni; *vāyuḥ* – Vāyu; *indraḥ* – Indra; *te* – they; *hi* – because; *enat* – this (*yakṣa*); *nediṣṭham* – from the closest; *paspṛśuḥ* – contacted, came in touch; *te* – they; *hi* – because; *enat* – this (*yakṣa*); *prathamaḥ* – first; *vidāñcakāra* – knew; *brahma iti* – as Brahman

Therefore, Agni, Vāyu and Indra, excel the other *deva*s for, they came in touch with the *yakṣa* from the closest place. They first came to know this *yakṣa* to be Brahman.

Here, we have to connect the *adhidaiva* properly. A sense organ is also called *deva* because it is effulgent, lighting up its own object. The lord of the senses is the *buddhi*, and Indra being the lord of the *deva*s is looked upon as the *buddhi*. The *vastu*, being *śrotrasya śrotraṁ cakṣuṣaścakṣuḥ manaso manaḥ*, cannot be objectified by the sense organs and the *buddhi*; they cannot help in gaining the knowledge of Brahman.

At the same time, Brahman is *prasiddha*, evident. It is like the *yakṣa* whom the *devatā*s saw right in front of them, but could not know it. Similarly, Brahman is evident, as the self in the form of '*aham*, I'. It is *asmat-pratyaya-gocara*, the subject matter of the I-thought. Therefore, the *śāstra* does not present Brahman as something other than myself. When I say, 'I am' then as 'I' Brahman is evident. This self-evident 'I' is not known as Brahman. Not only is it not known, it is also mistaken. The attempts of the *buddhi* to know Brahman are not going to be fruitful because, Brahman is the mind of the mind, and therefore cannot be thought of by the mind. At the same time, it is known as the consciousness that is manifest in every cognition, *pratibodha-viditam.*

The invariable in every cognition is the *svarūpa* of Brahman, and the variable manifestation of Brahman is the *jagat*, which includes your body, mind and senses also. That Brahman is indeed you; that is the teaching.

When this is true with reference to your mind and senses, then it is also true with reference to *devatā*s like Indra, Agni, and Vāyu. Whatever is valid in this *jīva* is valid in the *devatā* also. By becoming a *devatā* there is no automatic gain of *mokṣa*. Even the *devatā*s whom we worship are Brahman, but every *devatā* has to recognise this fact. Indra, Agni and Vāyu gained *mokṣa* because Umā taught them the *brahma vidyā*. Even they required *śruti*; you also need the same *śruti*. That is the idea conveyed here.

The *devatā*s are only exalted *jīva*s in exalted *upādhi*s. All of them are Īśvara, no doubt, but as Indra, Agni, Vāyu and so on, they are only *jīva*s with the predominance of *sattva-guṇa*. Therefore, just one statement is enough for them to gain the knowledge of Brahman. If your *antaḥkaraṇa* is also ready, then just one statement is enough for you too. So, the *mantra* also points out the *adhikāritva*, the qualification, for knowledge here.

Tataḥ eva vidāñcakāra:[61] From the teaching alone they came to know, because they were ready for it. But, they had to be taught. One cannot stumble upon it because it is oneself; it has to be revealed.

Īśvara himself is not the teacher really because he is you. Brahman appeared as Īśvara in the form of the *yakṣa* and went away. What came in his place is *brahma-vidyā,* the *pramāṇa* that gives the knowledge. How do we come to know that Umā is *brahma-vidyā?* Śaṅkara answers this question in his *bhāṣya* saying that it is because she was responsible for Indra's knowledge.[62] What we need for this knowledge is only *pramāṇa.*

Agni and Vāyu, not knowing themselves, went to the *yakṣa* in order to find out who he was. They should first ask, 'Who am I?' Instead, they wanted to ask the *yakṣa,* 'Who are you?' That is why the *yakṣa* shot back, "Tell me first who you are," for he knew their intention.

The question, '*ko 'si,* who are you?' is very relevant here. "Without knowing yourself you come and ask me." Then how can I know myself? You require *brahma vidyā.* Īśvara's grace is *brahma-vidyā.* Indra's prayer accounted for Īśvara's grace which is instrumental in providing the *pramāṇa.* And *pramāṇa* takes care of

---

[61] The verb should be in plural विदाञ्चक्रुः। The singluar usage is *chāndasam.*

[62] इन्द्रस्य बोधहेतुत्वाद् विद्यैव उमा। (केन. वाक्यभाष्यम् ४.१)

the knowledge. That it has to be gained by a *pramāṇa* employed by a teacher, is the main idea conveyed here.

Agni, the deity of speech, the words, could not know and came back. When Indra went, the *yakṣa* disappeared once and for all. Indra is taken as the mind because he is *indriyāṇāṁ rājā,* lord of the senses. The mind attempted to know but failed. *Yato vāco nivartante aprāpya manasā saḥ,* along with the mind—having not accomplished, having not understood what that Brahman is—the words came back. It means that they cannot objectify it.

The whole *śāstra* talks about the fact that Brahman is not objectified. It is of the nature of the subject, the truth of the subject, and therefore it has to be known through the *pramāṇa.* This is very well brought out in this story. Indra and others got enlightenment. Now they are all worshipped and all the worship goes to Īśvara. Previously they thought the worship they got, the victory they gained and the praise they received were because of them. Now, they do not have that notion anymore, having recognised that everything belongs to Īśvara. Knowing that Brahman, they are *atitarām iva,* definitely more exalted than other *devatā*s. Indra came back and taught Agni and Vāyu. They also became exalted then. The word, *iva* is in the sense of emphasis, *eva.* So, this knowledge alone makes the difference. It is Brahman because of which all the *deva*s are glorious. If the *deva*s recognise, 'I am Brahman,' they become the source of all glories. Indeed, all these *devatās* are the most exalted now.

Who are they? *Yad agnirvāyurindraḥ*, these three deities—Indra, Agni and Vāyu. Why are they more exalted? Because *te hi enad nediṣṭhaṁ paspṛśuḥ*: they came to know intimately, *nediṣṭham* Brahman. The word '*prathama*' meaning 'first' is an adverb qualifying the verb *vidāñcakāra*, knew. The plural word '*te*' indicates other *deva*s who might have been taught. The word *prathama* also points out this. If they came to know first, that means other *deva*s were also taught later. Otherwise the word 'first' is not necessary. They did not keep it as a secret. Since they came to know first, they are definitely greater.

Once I gain this knowledge, even though there is no *guru*, there is no *śiṣya*, still, the fact remains that I received this knowledge from this person, and as long as this *upādhi*—the body-mind-sense complex—is alive, the respect, is always given to the *guru*. Here also the *deva*s who gained this knowledge first are offered salutations because they are *guru*s.

Among these three, Indra, Agni and Vāyu, Indra is more exalted than the other two, because he is the *guru* for the other two. He definitely occupies a better place; that is pointed out here.

Mantra 3

तस्माद्वा इन्द्रोऽतितरामिव अन्यान्देवान्। स ह्येनन्नेदिष्ठं पस्पर्श। स ह्येनत्प्रथमो विदाञ्चकार ब्रह्मेति॥ ४.३॥

tasmād vā indro'titarām iva anyān devān, sa hyenannediṣṭhaṁ pasparśa, sa hyenat prathamo vidāñcakāra brahmeti. (4.3)

tasmāt – therefore; *vai* – indeed; *indraḥ* – Indra; *atitarām iva*[63] – indeed/certainly is more exalted; *anyān* – (than) the other (two); *devān*–*devas*; *saḥ* – he; *hi* – indeed; *enat* – this (*yakṣa*); *nediṣṭham* – from the closest; *pasparśa* – came in touch; *saḥ* – he; *hi* – indeed; *enat* – this; *prathamaḥ* – first; *vidāñcakāra* – knew; *brahma*– the (*yakṣa*) to be Brahman; *iti* – thus

Therefore, Indra indeed is more exalted than the other (two) *devas*. He indeed came in touch with this (*yakṣa*) from the closest (place) and he indeed knew first this (*yakṣa*) to be Brahman.

Since Indra taught this knowledge to Agni and Vāyu, he remains the most exalted among all the *devas*.

---

[63] इन्द्रः अत्यन्तमेव श्रेष्ठत्वेन वर्तते इति शेषः। (केन भाष्यम्)

Indra (remains) certainly more exalted. The word 'remains' is to be supplied.

Not only that. Indra excels all the other *deva*s because *sa hi enad nediṣṭhaṁ pasparśa,* he came in close contact with the *yakṣa,* by the grace of the same *yakṣa,* in the form of *brahma-vidyā.* He was the first one to receive this knowledge and therefore he is the most exalted among them. Even though all the other *deva*s who received this knowledge are *jñānin*s, still, Indra continues to be recipient of worship from the other *deva*s.

This interesting story implies that these *deva*s, like Indra, could not and did not know until they were taught. At the same time, the *vastu,* Brahman, as *ātman* is *prasiddha.* The same Brahman as Īśvara is *prasiddha* in the form of all that is here. Still it is *jñeya,* to be known. It is *sāmānyena prasiddhaḥ,* in general it is evident as, 'I am,' but *viśeṣataḥ,* in particular, it is not known as limitless. It is exactly like the rope-snake. In the rope-snake example, what is perceived as 'this' is *prasiddha.* But then, the object is not understood as it is. If you do not know the object which is evident, referred by the word 'this', then the *ādhāra,*[64] the locus where you commit the mistake, would join your wrong perception, 'this is snake.'

By knowledge of the object, I do not really come to know the *ādhāra,* the locus—it is already known.

---

[64] *Idaṁ-pratyaya-viṣayam, idantayā yad vastu gṛhyate tad ādhāram,* that which is perceived by you as 'this' object is called *ādhāra,* the locus.

In the wake knowledge, what is mistaken goes away. 'This' as rope remains. Therefore, *ādhāra* continues. I saw the snake because the snake has its *adhiṣṭhāna*,[65] the unperceived rope. In the wake of the knowledge of the *adhiṣṭhāna* the superimposed object disappears. 'This' joins the *adhiṣṭhāna* for one to say, 'this is rope.'

The self-evident *ātman* 'I am' is the *ādhāra*, the locus, for me to commit a mistake. Therefore, there is this conclusion—I am a *saṁsārin*, subject to limitations, pain, sorrow and so on. The *saṁsārin* is a superimposition. In the vision of the *śruti* 'I am' is *satyaṁ jñānam anantaṁ brahma.* I do not know this fact, and therefore, I commit the mistake of taking myself to be a *saṁsārin.* It is this *saṁsārin* who goes about knowing things and that is good enough to conduct his or her life. But the *saṁsārin* has no *pramāṇa* at all to know that he or she is *satyaṁ jñānam anantaṁ brahma.* Brahman cannot be objectified because Brahman is the very *svarūpa*, the *adhiṣṭhāna* of the *saṁsārin.* The knowledge of the *adhiṣṭhāna* is *viśeṣa-jñāna.* To gain that knowledge alone is one's pursuit of *pramāṇa.* One is not searching for the *ādhāra,* one is searching only for the *adhiṣṭhāna* in terms of knowledge.

---

65 *Yasya jñānena āropitavastu nivartate tad adhiṣṭhānam,* in the wake of which knowledge the mistaken object disappears is called *adhiṣṭhāna.*

The knowledge that the self-evident *ātman* is Brahman takes place as a result of one's exposure to the *śruti pramāṇa*. Our pursuit is only to gain the knowledge of the *adhiṣṭhāna* which removes the *samsāritva* superimposed on the *ātman*, the *ādhāra*.

The story is narrated only to tell what exactly happens when one wants to 'see' Brahman. Indra went to Brahman; it disappeared from his sight. Why? Because *yaccakṣuṣā na paśyati yena cakṣūṁṣi paśyati*—that by whose presence the eyes see, and itself one does not see by the eyes, is Brahman. Eyes cannot directly see that source of light because of which alone, the eyes can see. The eyes cannot directly see the sunlight; they can only see the reflected light. That is the example of lightning that comes in the next *mantra*. Like a flash of lightning, Indra thought he saw the *yakṣa, saguṇa* Brahman. But when he wanted to know it, the *yakṣa*, disappeared like a lightning. Then he has to be taught what exactly is the *svarūpa* of the *yakṣa*.

What is evident is to be taught. The evident becomes non-evident like the lightning that appears and disappears. This example of lightning follows now.

Mantra 4

तस्यैष आदेशो यदेतद्विद्युतो व्यद्युतदा ३ इतीन्न्यमी-
मिषदा ३ इत्यधिदैवतम् ॥ ४.४ ॥

tasyaiṣa ādeśo yad etad vidyuto vyadyutad ā itīnnyamīmiṣad ā ityadhidaivatam. (4.4)

tasya – of that (Brahman) *eṣaḥ* – this; *ādeśaḥ* – teaching; *yad* – which; *etad* – this (Brahman); *vidyutaḥ* – of the lightning; *vyadyutad* – flashed; *ā* – (this Brahman) is comparable; *iti*– thus; *it* – and; *nyamīmiṣat* – closed (the eyes); *ā* – (this Brahman) is comparable; *iti* – thus (ends); *adhidaivatam* – (the teaching) centred on the *devas*.

The following is the teaching of that Brahman (through comparison): This Brahman is likened to a flash of the lightning, thus (is the first teaching). This Brahman is comparable to the blinking of the eyes, thus (is the second teaching). Thus (ends) the teaching centred on the *devas*.

Knowing Brahman is like seeing a flash of lightning. *Parokṣa-jñāna,* mediate knowledge of Brahman is not possible because there is no other Brahman presented by *śāstra*, except the consciousness that is oneself. One's *śraddhā* that Brahman exists can be called *parokṣa-jñāna,* even though *parokṣa-jñāna* is really inferential knowledge. When one sees smoke on the distant hill, one infers that there is fire; this is indirect knowledge. It is final and conclusive if the inferential basis is free from any defect. This is called *parokṣa-jñāna*.

There is no *parokṣa-jñāna* of Brahman, because Brahman happens to be you. If we accept a *parokṣa-jñāna* of Brahman, it is the loss of the self. In his *Pañcadaśī,* Vidyāraṇya says that in one place that, "It is equivalent to the loss of the capital for the one who wanted its growth."[66] One goes to the *sāstra* with a desire to know *ātman* and learns that the self is '*parokṣaṁ brahma.*' That means you are losing yourself. Brahman-knowledge is *aparokṣa. Aparokṣa* means not *parokṣa* but self-evident. "I am a *saṁsārin,* subject to happiness and sorrow," is not an inferred fact; you directly experience it.

I am always *nitya-aparokṣaṁ brahma.* There is no way of my missing myself being Brahman. Even if I do not know, I am Brahman. That is a fact that I have to know. Here is an *upamā upadeśaḥ,* teaching through an example, and the example is lightning.

Tasya eṣa ādeśaḥ: This is the teaching through an illustration of that Brahman which was understood by Indra and the other *devatās*. What is that? *Yad etad*

---

[66] *vṛddhim iṣṭavato mūlam api naṣṭam itī dṛśam* (7.86)

vidyutaḥ vyadyutad ā (3). The vowel *ā* is *pluta,* having three *mātrās*, units of length, in pronunciation. The meaning of this *pluta*[67] is in the sense of '*iva,* like'. It indicates the *upamā,* illustration. Sometimes it can indicate the sense of questioning, like in *kaścana gacchatī* (3), in *Taittirīyopaniṣad.*[68] Here, it is in the sense of illustration—*vidyutaḥ vyadyutad ā* (3), like a flash of *vyadyutad,* read as *vidyotanam,* lightning. Brahman is compared to lightning because when Indra wanted to know, Brahman just disappeared like the flash of lightning. One cannot directly see the lightning; it blinds the eyes. One can only see a reflection on the clouds. Similarly, Brahman disappears from the inquiring mind of Indra. That means, even a *devatā* cannot get to know Brahman by perception, inference and so on. The *devatā* has to be taught, as was Indra by Umā.

Here, one may object, 'I see the lightning, but I do not see Brahman'. The example cited is not to reveal Brahman as an object. Brahman cannot be objectified because it is of the nature of *ātman.* What Indra saw was not really Brahman. He saw Īśvara in a particular form, the *yakṣa,* and he wanted to know the truth of that form. But the form just disappeared like lightning. That is the example given here. Brahman is unlike everything else. There is no example for Brahman.

---

67 *upamārthe plutaḥ*

68 *Mantra* 2.6

To give such an example one has to find out something outside Brahman, but there is nothing outside Brahman. Everything is Brahman.[69] So, the example here is meant to confirm that it is not an object for the senses and other means of knowledge.

Iti it nyamīmiṣad ā: Like (lightning) closes (your) eyes. You cannot see lightning; only that much is the example. The word *iti*[70] is to point out the *ādeśa,* teaching. The word '*it*'[71] means 'and'. When you look at lightning, the eyes close automatically. They do not consult you. If the eyes were to close after making a decision, then by the time your mind decides, you will be blind. Just as you cannot keep your eyes open, and look at the lightning to find out how bright it is, so too, when you want to see Brahman, the mind makes a retreat. Brahman disappears from your vicinity. If you want to see some form for *upāsanā,* it is available but the *svarūpa* of Brahman is not available at all for seeing.

Iti adhidaivatam: This is the teaching with reference to the *deva*s, the story of the *deva*s. Brahman is that in whose presence alone the *deva*s are *deva*s, and whom the *deva*s could not understand, unless taught. That is the whole subject matter.

---

[69] *sarvaṁ khalvidaṁ brahma* (*Chāndogyopaniṣad* 3.14.1).

[70] इति शब्दः आदेश-प्रतिनिर्देशार्थः । इति अयम् आदेशः इति । (केन भाष्यम्)

[71] इत् शब्दः समुच्चयार्थः । (केन भाष्यम्)

In reality the *adhidaivata* and the *adhyātma* are manifest Brahman as the total and the individual. Both do not have being and power of their own and both need to know Brahman through *śabda-pramāṇa*.

Mantra 5

अथाध्यात्मम्। यदेतद्गच्छतीव च मनोऽनेन चैतदुपस्मरत्यभीक्ष्णꣳसङ्कल्पः ॥ ४.५ ॥

athādhyātmam, yad etad gacchatīva ca mano'nena caitad upasmaratyabhīkṣṇaṁ saṅkalpaḥ. (4.5)

atha – now follows; *adhyātmam* – (the teaching of Brahman) centred on the individual; *yad etad* – this Brahman; *gacchati iva* – appear(s) to move towards; *ca* – and; *manaḥ* – the thought(s); *anena* – through this; *ca* – and; *etad* – this Brahman; *upasmarati* – one recognises; *abhīkṣṇam* – repeatedly; *saṅkalpaḥ* – meditation (on this Brahman)

Now follows (the teaching of Brahman) centred on the individual. The thoughts appear to move towards (reveal as it were) this Brahman and one recognises this Brahman through the thoughts and meditates repeatedly (on this Brahman).

With reference to the individual, the *vastu* is *śrotrasya śrotram*, etc., by whose presence alone the senses and mind have their existence and function, and whom the senses and the mind cannot know. To know this truth that the individual is Brahman, there is no other way except an external means of knowledge, that is, the teaching of the *upaniṣad*.

Atha adhyātmam:[72] Here, with reference to *pratyagātman* the teaching is given. The topic for which *ātman* is the *adhikaraṇa*, the subject matter, is called *adhyātma*. The prefix *adhi* points out the subject matter. What is the teaching?

Yad etat: That Brahman is this. *Yat* is *prakṛtaṁ brahma*, Brahman which has been under discussion, which the *deva*s knew after being taught. For gaining the knowledge of that Brahman alone, the *śāstra* now engages itself. That *jñeyaṁ brahma* is *etad*, this *pratyagātma-vastu*. *Etat*, 'this' means the *ātman* that is always self evident, self-revealing.

Manaḥ gacchati iva: The mind goes, as though, towards Brahman that is the self. Agni, Vāyu and Indra went very near Brahman, as though. They did not understand then. Similarly here, the mind goes, as though, towards this Brahman because it has to know. Anything that the mind has to know, it has to

---

72 *pratyagātma-viṣaya-ādeśaḥ – pratyagātmā eva viṣyaḥ yasya saḥ ādeśaḥ* – the teaching (*ādeśaḥ*) whose subject matter is the innermost self.

go towards and objectify. If a flower is to be known, the mind has to objectify the flower and assume the form of a flower.

Now Brahman has to be known. However, we cannot know Brahman like we know the flower. We come to know a flower because of Brahman which is the self-revealing *ātman*. So there is no question of the mind going towards Brahman, and revealing Brahman. You do not require to reveal that Brahman because of which everything is revealed. But to remove the ignorance of the fact that *pratyagātman* is *satyaṁ jñānam anantaṁ brahma,* a *vṛtti* has to take place in the mind. There is no other activity involved. In knowledge of a flower, the flower *vṛtti* removes the flower ignorance. Then, you say, 'This is a flower,' 'I know this flower.' The remoteness of the flower is removed by the *vṛtti,* and then the object of the *vṛtti* is recognised by you, the subject, the knower, who stands apart from the recognised object. Your relating to the object as the knower of the object is called *phala-vyāpti*. But, in the case of knowledge of Brahman, the *vṛtti* created by the teaching 'You are that', removes the ignorance of the fact of *ātman* being Brahman, and thereafter, the *phala-vyāpti* is neither possible nor necessary because the self-revealing 'I' is Brahman. Some people overlook the fact that one requires the mind to have any knowledge. When questioned further, they will say that it is a different type of mind. This is due to not understanding clearly what is *satyaṁ brahma* and what is *mithyā*. When one commits one mistake, one has to cover that mistake by a series of mistakes.

One does not transcend the mind. In fact, the mind is required, and that is said in this *mantra*. *Manaḥ gacchati iva,* the mind as though goes towards Brahman at the time of *śravaṇa*. The same mind recognises Brahman. *Pratibodha-viditam,* in every thought, consciousness is invariable and this recognition, in the form of a *vṛtti,* is gained only by the mind. This is the *śravaṇa-phala*.

Then, what is the result of *manana*? If there is a doubt in this recognition—how can I be Brahman—that doubt has to be removed by the same faculty, the mind that creates it. The doubt has come because of some fallacious thinking and one has to see the fallacy in that thinking and remove the doubt. That is where logic is used.

A person has doubts because of reason. Unless there is reason, there cannot be a doubt. And false conclusions are based on wrong reasoning. Such a person is basically weak even though he or she is armed with the stick of reason. Like even a weak person comes out with a stick in hand to fight a strong person who has no stick. The strong wrenches the stick from the weak and beats him with the same stick. Similarly, with the same stick of reason, the fallacious reasoning that created the doubt is removed by valid reasoning. One then gains firm knowledge. This process is called *manana*.

Reason is also used in analysing the *śruti* and finding out what it wants to convey, what is its *tātparya*, vision. What is said by the *śruti* should not be against reason. Suppose the *śruti* says that one gains *amṛtatva* in heaven. If heaven, *svarga*, is another place, it is bound by time—the one who makes it to heaven is bound to leave. There is no possibility of *amṛtatva*, eternal life. Either we give a meaning for the word *svarga* that will go with *amṛtatva* or interpret the word, '*amṛtatva*' to mean absence of the ageing process as long as one lives in *svarga*. Because one is committed to heaven as an end, the *śruti* sometimes talks in the same language and points out, 'That end called heaven is you.' Therefore, we try to understand what is the *vivakṣā* of the *śruti*. That is what is done in *śravaṇa*. The result of *śravaṇa* is *tātparya-niścaya*, clear knowledge, if one is an *adhikārin*.

The *vastu* is already revealed by the *śāstra* and that has to stay. The *vastu* is not established or proved by reason. If by reason the *vastu* has to be established then, it becomes an object of inference and it becomes *parokṣa*. One cannot, therefore, say Vedanta is logical or scientific. Reasoning is used to eliminate all contentions and doubts with reference to one being Brahman, revealed by the *śāstra*. If this is understood, then one's attitude and approach towards the *śāstra* itself are different.

Therefore, *anenaiva manasā mumukṣuḥ puruṣaḥ samīpataḥ etad brahma upasmarati iva smaraṇaṁ karoti iva*, by this mind alone, the seeker contemplates intimately, as it were, upon this Brahman. The word *iva* has to be added after *upasmarati*. The importance of the mind in knowing the *vastu* is pointed out here. It was said earlier, *mataṁ yasya na veda saḥ*, the one who thinks that it is known, does not know. From this one may conclude that it is beyond the mind. The *śruti* removes that conclusion here. Agni, Vāyu, and Indra could not know, not because it was beyond knowing, but because they wanted to know Brahman as an object. It cannot be known by the mind as an object of knowledge. But the mind is necessary. *Upasmarati*[73] means *brahma aham asmi iti nidhidyhāsanaṁ karoti*, he contemplates as 'I am Brahman'. Brahman is, as though, objectified by him; the mind goes, as it were, to Brahman. For instance, 'This is a flower' when I say, you recognise the flower; 'this is a tree' when I say, you recognise the tree. When I say, *pūrṇaṁ brahma*, the mind seems to appreciate that; the mind goes, as it were, towards the meaning of the words *pūrṇaṁ brahma*. That is what is said here and also extended further. That flower also is Brahman; the tree also is Brahman. They are non-separate from Brahman which is you, *caitanyātman*, consciousness, the self. When you

---

[73] *upa samīpataḥ san smarati.*

contemplate repeatedly upon the *vastu*, the mind stays in the recognition. Therefore, it is said *anenaiva upasmarati iva.*

The meaning of the word *upasmarati* can include *manana* also since removal of any doubt regarding the *vastu* is also involved. One more reason for taking the meaning of *upasmarati* as *manana* is the presence of words in the sentence *abhīkṣṇaṁ saṅkalpaḥ* which means *nididhyāsana*. This *saṅkalpa* also is done by the mind alone. There is no action really speaking, it is *iva,* meaning, 'as though'.

There is a *mantra* in the *Bṛhadāraṇyaka Upaniṣad,*[74] *dhyāyati iva lelāyati iva. Dhyāyati iva* means the person as though contemplates upon Brahman. Why? Because he went away from Brahman, as though; only then is 'as though' meditation possible. If going away from Brahman is real, then there is no question of Brahman being limitless. The mind, recognising the invariable, as though contemplates, *dhyāyati iva*. When the mind is totally concerned with the variable, then you are away from Brahman, as though. You need not bring the mind to Brahman. *Lelāyati iva,* wherever the mind has moved away, there you recognise the invariable; there itself is your *samādhi,* contemplation. It was already revealed that the invariable, being what it is, is ever present and it is recognised as such.

---

[74] *Mantra* 4.3.7

We have to note that there is no need to move away from an object, but rather stay with the object and recognise the invariable. One good thing about the mind is that it keeps on moving from object to object; never stays with one object. This makes it easy for one to recognise the invariable. Suppose one thinks of a pot and one's thought is stuck with the pot; one then cannot recognise the invariable from the variable. When the thought moves, one can see the invariable. This recognition of the invariable among the variables is the *abhīkṣṇaṁ saṅkalpaḥ.* It is 'as though' the mind goes to the invariable.

Abhīkṣṇam means always. Until you require no more contemplation, you contemplate. The question of how long I have to contemplate is meaningless. The question, 'how long?' is relevant only when the task is something bitter or painful. Contemplating, "I am Brahman" is like a sugar crystal remaining in sugar syrup.

Mantra 6

तद्ध तद्वनं नाम । तद्वनमित्युपासितव्यम् । स य एतदेवं
वेदाभि हैनꣳसर्वाणि भूतानि संवाञ्छन्ति ॥ ४.६ ॥

taddha tadvanaṁ nāma, tadvanam ityupāsitavyam,
sa ya etad evaṁ vedābhi hainaṁ̐ sarvāṇi bhūtāni
saṁvāñchanti (4.6)

tad – that (Brahman); *ha* – indeed; *tadvanam* – adorable among all the beings; *nāma* – well known; *tadvanam* – the adorable one among all; *iti* – thus; *upāsitavyam* – (that Brahman) has to be meditated upon; *saḥ yaḥ* – whoever; *etad* – this (Brahman); *evam* – in this manner; *veda* – meditates; *ha* – indeed; *enam*– him; *sarvāṇi* – all; *bhūtāni* – beings; *abhisaṁ-vāñchanti* – adore

Indeed that Brahman is well known as the adorable one among all the beings. (Therefore, Brahman) has to be meditated upon as the adorable one among all. All beings adore that person who meditates upon this Brahman in this manner.

At the beginning of the third section it was said that this Brahman alone, as Īśvara, was the cause of the victory of *deva*s. The *deva*s due to conceit became very proud. Īśvara thought, 'I will reveal the truth to them,' and appeared in the form of a *yakṣa*. Later, as Umā, Īśvara revealed the truth that is Brahman. After the teaching, Indra now says, 'All the worship that I receive go to Īśvara, because he is *vanam*,[75] the most glorious, the worshipful.

The mind, the senses of a *jīva* as well as those of Indra and other *devatā*s—all of them draw their

---

[75] *vananīyam, pūjanīyam*–one who is to be worshipped

existence from Īśvara alone. Therefore, the source, the repository of all glories is only one, and that is Īśvara. Lord Kṛṣṇa in the *Bhagavad Gītā*, Chapter 10, tells:[76] "All the *vibhūti*, glories of individuals and objects belong to me, they come from me." In fact, anything that exists with its own special characteristics is a manifestation of Īśvara. Therefore, the status enjoyed by the *deva*s as the presiding deities of the various laws is another glory of Īśvara alone. Indra being the presiding deity of all the *deva*s is due to Īśvara. Vāyu being a deity of strength is due to Īśvara, and Agni being a deity of speech is, again, due to Īśvara. Because of Īśvara they are what they are.

Tad ha tadvanam: That (Brahman) is, *ha*, indeed, known as *tadvanam*. Brahman as Īśvara gains this name *tadvanam*,[77] the one who is to be adored, who is the most worshipful, who can be an object of *upāsanā*.

Here, *upāsanā* means recognising the glory of Brahman in the form of this world. In the process,

---

76 *yadyad vibhūtimat-sattvam śrīmad-ūrjitam eva vā, tattad evāvagaccha tvaṁ mama tejoṁśa-sambhavam* (*Bhagavad Gītā* 10.41)

Whatever existent thing there is, which has glory, which is endowed with any form of wealth, or that which is mighty, every one of that, may you know, is born of a fraction of my glory.

77 तस्य प्राणिजातस्य प्रत्यगात्मभूतत्वाद् वनं वननीयं सम्भजनीयम् अतः तद्वनम् नाम । (केन भाष्यम्) – Being the inner self of all beings, it is worshipful; therefore, it is called *tadvanam*.

Brahman becomes the one who is glorious and the appreciation of this glory makes one's ego imbued with the presence of Īśvara, thereby transforming the ego from its alienation to be one connected to Īśvara. Therefore, at the level of *upāsanā* itself, one gains freedom from misery.

A word-form similar to *vananīyam* is *vareṇyam* in the *gāyatrī mantra.*[78] The actual *mantra* minus the *vyāhṛtis* begins with *om tat savituḥ vareṇyam. Tad vareṇyam* has the same meaning as *tadvanam. Om,* Brahman alone, is all the three worlds. Every glory therein is the glory of Brahman. Therefore, Brahman gains the name *tadvanam, tad vareṇyam.*

When one sings the glory of his or her own *iṣṭa-devatā,* the praise of that glory goes only to Īśvara. Just as all the rivers go and merge in the ocean, similarly, all forms of prayers coming from different religious cultures, reach the same Īśvara alone. In whichever form people invoke, in that form Īśvara comes to bless.[79] Therefore, Īśvara is *tadvanam.*

Tadvanam iti upāsitavyam. Nāma-saṅkīrtana is a kind of *upāsanā* wherein you repeat the names of Īśvara and

---

[78] *Gāyatrī* is the name of a metre. This particular *mantra* of 24 syllables is in this *gāyatrī* metre, used only by the Veda. Among the *mantras* in the *gāyatrī* metre, the *sāvitrī mantra*, which we call *gāyatrī,* is the most popular, and occurs in all the Vedas.

[79] *Ye yathā māṁ prapadyante tāṁstathaiva bhajāmyaham...* (*Bhagavad Gītā* 4.11)

sing in praise of him. Every name reveals Īśvara's glory; there is no flattery when you glorify Īśvara. In fact, any glory mentioned is always understood by us less than what it is. With our limited mind we understand *ananta*, limitless, without really knowing what is *ananta*. In fact, we understand the limitless as one free from limitation. Through the method of negation alone we can understand it. Can we ever say anything more than what Īśvara is? Flattery is saying something more than what the person is. So we cannot flatter Īśvara. This is *nāma-saṅkīrtana.*

In doing *arcanā*[80] with 108 or 1008 names, the glories of Īśvara are said. After every name you say, '*namaḥ,* my salutation unto you.' In each name the word *namaḥ* is crucial and is connected to Īśvara and me. The ego has its own areas through which it tries to establish itself as an entity, and it holds on to them with the sense, 'This is me'. Saying, "*namaḥ,* my salutation unto him," loosens this hold. Here the word, '*namaḥ*' goes along with a specific word in dative case one after another. Like you say, '*acyutāya namaḥ,* unto *acyuta,* one who does not have any kind of decline in terms of time, my salutation; *anantāya namaḥ,* unto *ananta,* the limitless, my salutation. I think I am *cyuta,* who is subject to decline, old age, and then disappearance. When I do *namaskāra* to *acyuta,* I am

---

[80] It is a step in doing *pūjā* in which one offers flowers at the altar chanting different names of the Lord.

not alienated from him. Here, *namaḥ* is at the devotee level. This *namaḥ* is taken further, in the wake of understanding of the non-dual reality of Īśvara; now there is only *acyuta*. His glory is my glory. Here, surrender is a complete gain. The altar of surrender is very important. If you surrender to someone who is lesser than you, you lose.

Bhīṣma gives out *Viṣṇu Sahasranāma* in the *Mahābhārata* from his deathbed. He also gives *Śiva Sahasranāma.* In whichever area I find myself lacking, there I take to the glory of Īśvara. I seek bonding with him, and I get connected in that area, and the ego becomes secure. That is where these elaborate 108 or 1008 names of Īśvara are useful; each one of them has to be understood properly. One becomes the recipient of the blessing of Īśvara in that particular form. In these names Īśvara is presented as both the father and mother. There is a male as well as a female aspect in everybody. If there is a place where the fusion of both these aspects takes place, it is Īśvara, because both the *śakti* and the wielder of *śakti*, representing the female and male aspects, are one and the same Īśvara.

The *arcanā, nāma-saṅkīrtana* and so on have their basis in the words *tadvana-nāma-upāsanā.* They are the expansion of the *śāstra*, because the nucleus is there. When one understands their significance, one's act of worship gains direction.

The very act of worship is nothing but showing respect in adoration. First it is an act of respect. Then the respect becomes an act of worship because the altar of respect happens to be Īśvara. I relate to Īśvara through this act of worship. Here, that worship is called *upāsanā*. *Upāsitavyam* means definitely that Īśvara has to be worshipped through *guṇa-abhidhāna*, specific attributes. In the language of a devotee, Īśvara is looked upon as *ananta-kalyāṇa-guṇa-sampanna*, the one whohas all the virtues in an absolute measure.

One can meditate upon Īśvara with eyes closed, and also with eyes open. When one sees the glory of Īśvara in a flower, it definitely has to do with much more than mere sight. It is purely mental. One appreciates the glory of Īśvara because of whom a flower is a flower, the eye is an eye, the mind is a mind, and a *devatā* is a *devatā*.

What does one get from this? One gets Īśvara by one's side; the separation goes away. If one needs help, one has to go to the right person. If one seeks the help of somebody who requires help, then one does not know whether one is holding the person or the person is holding one. One has to help oneself with Īśvara and better one helps oneself; that is the truth about the person. Rāvaṇa also took help from Īśvara, but not very intelligently. One also has to take help from Īśvara intelligently. That is what Īśvara is about. Īśvara is always available, right inside, outside, everywhere; one has to tap.

In this *upāsanā*, it looks as though I sell myself out. After all, I do require some glories for my self-image. If all my glories belong to Īśvara, will I not become an empty shell? Is this not a sell-out? No. By doing so, only one's smallness goes; the glories do not go. We see all the glory belonging to Īśvara.

Yaḥ etad (*brahma*) *evam* (*upāsitavyam*) *veda* (*upāste*): The one who meditates on Brahman as *tad-vanam* in this manner—that every glory belongs to Īśvara—*sarvāṇi bhūtāni saṁvāñchanti* all beings love to be in the presence of that person. One does not seek any more approval of others.

People always seek someone who is strong. This is the strength. You are strong only when you have Īśvara as your strength. To get this strength by your side you have to simply claim Īśvara. Īśvara will not decide to come to you. He does not require coming to you; he has already come to you. You have to claim it. We are told of *āśrama*s where even the animals live without any fear. They sense safety because the persons living there are free from fear of being hurt by them.

Strength is nothing but one's freedom from manipulating, freedom from taking advantage of a situation. Readiness to give and yield; that is strength, inner strength.

The one who worships Īśvara in the form of glory becomes such a glory that all people love to be with this person. The prefix *abhi* should be taken along with the verb *saṁvāñchanti. Abhitaḥ saṁvāñchanti* means people like to be with that person all the time. They never get tired of that person; in fact, all the more they want to be with that person, because he is like Īśvara.

Mantra 7

The teacher now feels the teaching is over, and takes a moment out when a student gets up and makes a request:

उपनिषदं भो ब्रूहीत्युक्ता त उपनिषद्ब्राह्मी वाव त उपनिषदमब्रूमेति ॥ ४.७ ॥

upaniṣadaṁ bho brūhītyuktā ta upaniṣad brāhmī vāva ta upaniṣadam abrūmeti. (4.7)

upaniṣadam – the *upaniṣad; bhoḥ* – O Teacher! *brūhi* – please teach; *iti* – thus; *uktā* – has been taught; *te* – to you; *upaniṣad* – the *upaniṣad; brāhmī* – that which reveals Brahman; *vāva* – indeed; *te* – to you; *upaniṣadam* – the *upaniṣad; abrūma* – I have taught; *iti* – thus

"O Teacher! Please teach (me) the *upaniṣad,*" (the student asked). (The teacher replied), "The *upaniṣad* has been taught to you (by me).

(Till now) I have taught you the *upaniṣad* which reveals Brahman indeed."

Bhoḥ upaniṣadaṁ brūhi: Sir, please teach me *upaniṣad*. This teacher is great for he does not show any despair. On the contrary he says, *brāhmī*[81] *upaniṣad te uktā,* I have taught you the *upaniṣad* revealing Brahman. The *upaniṣad* that unfolds Brahman has already been said.

What is the idea behind the question? The *upaniṣad* creates an occasion for talking something more. The knowledge of *brahma-vidyā* itself is *mokṣa*. However, it is looked upon as a means, and *mokṣa* as the end. In the wake of one, the other happens, and therefore, we consider *jñāna* as a means for *mokṣa*. For *mokṣa* there is nothing else required other than this knowledge; that is revealed here. And for *jñāna* what is necessary is *pramāṇa,* as given here. Therefore, there is no other *sādhana-apekṣā,* dependence upon some other means, for *jñāna* to give its result, *mokṣa*. Neither does this knowledge need to be augmented by something else so that it can fructify in *mokṣa*.

This is unlike the knowledge of *karma,* a ritual. In the case of a ritual, one needs to have the knowledge of the ritual before it is performed. The *phala,* result, of the ritual is dependent upon the proper

---

[81] *Brahmaṇaḥ iyaṁ brāhmī. Brahma-viṣayā ityarthaḥ.* That which is connected to Brahman is *brāhmī*. It means that knowledge for which the subject matter is Brahman.

performance of the ritual. The knowledge of the ritual, even though born of *veda-pramāṇa,* is not conclusive; that is, it does not end up giving the result, even when you understand everything about that ritual. There is *kāraka-apekṣā,* dependence on factors necessary for performing a *karma,* for the result to fructify. Of them, the primary factor is *kartṛ,* the doer, who performs the *karma* with the aid of other factors, like instruments, and so on, to get the result.

Here, on the other hand, the very knowledge unfolded by the *śruti* is able to give one the *puruṣārtha,* which is *mokṣa.* What is *arthyate,* sought after, is not knowledge but *mokṣa,* though one may not recognise, 'I want *mokṣa.*' Honestly, everybody wants *mokṣa;* there is no choice here. Behind all the pursuits that one goes after, is the pursuit of *mokṣa.* The freedom centred on oneself is the end that is always kept in view which is self-knowledge. Like any other knowledge, it does not depend upon anything else except the appropriate *pramāṇa.* But this self-knowledge has certain special features, and that is where the preparedness comes in; the person must be capable of knowing. For instance, a person interested in a subject matter, and capable of knowing, cannot understand anything if the medium of teaching happens to be Sanskrit which the person does not know. The person will not know even if the best of teachers teaches. Therefore, the *antaḥkaraṇa,* the mind, should be prepared. *Saṁskṛta* means 'well prepared'.

A well prepared mind is necessary. A mind that has the linguistic *saṁskāra,* the education of the language is called *saṁskṛta-antaḥkaraṇa.*

Let us say the linguistic *saṁskāra* is there. The subject matter, 'I,' is already there, and nothing else is talked about which is beyond one's experience. The *upaniṣad* only talks about the 'I' and analyses one's pain, pleasure, one's dream, sleep, and waking—all these experiences that are very personal and highly intimate to oneself. The *ātman* is self-revealing. The statement, "I am a *saṁsārin,*" itself reveals the presence of the *ātman,* and therefore, nothing new is taught. Yet suppose, the knowledge does not take place when it is taught, it is clear that there is something else necessary here. A mature human being is required here. A mature human being is one who is objective, who is dispassionate, who is able to command compassion, understanding, readiness to reach out spontaneously, and being sensitive to others' pain. This preparedness is going to be stated as a prerequisite by the teacher. He says that he has already taught the *upaniṣad* without leaving anything to be desired. From this, it is clear that the one who asks is not a new entrant; he has been listening to the whole teaching. Therefore, the *upaniṣad* seems committed to convey two ideas through the student's question.

One is, you do not require anything more than *pramāṇa* for knowledge, because it says *upaniṣad te uktā,* the knowledge has been taught to you. Another idea is, for the result of *mokṣa* nothing else is necessary; the very *jñāna* is *mokṣa*. In the statement, the *upaniṣad* is taught in full, the *śruti* negates any connection of *karma* to knowledge. Some people do give *śeṣa-śeṣi-sambandha,* subsidiary-main connection, between knowledge and action. One is the main thing and the other supports the main thing. For them, *mokṣa* is an event that is going to happen later in some other world.

By presenting the student's question, the *śruti* herself seems to concede this particular predicament—that one may listen, and still one may not even gain an insight that one can, and ask, "Please teach me *upaniṣad*."

The question can be interpreted differently also, because the word *upaniṣad* has another meaning. A secret, *rahasya,* is called *upaniṣad*. Śaṅkara takes it that way. The teaching seems to have not worked for him, and so the student is asking, "Please tell me, is there any further secret?"[82]

---

82 किं पूर्वोक्त-उपनिषच्छेषतया तत्सहकारि साधनान्तरापेक्षा अथ निरपेक्षैव। सापेक्षा चेद् अपेक्षितविषयाम् उपनिषदं ब्रूहि। (केन भाष्यम्)

Is there anything else as a supporting means for *Upanisad* (knowledge to free one) or knowledge is dependent (means for freedom). If it needs supporting means, please tell the secret of that on which knowledge depends.

We see two types of *adhikārins* cited by the *upaniṣad*. One student was able to see what the teacher taught. He confirmed, '*manye viditam*, I consider (it) is known by me.' He also stated the manner of his knowing—*nāhaṁ manye suvedeti no na vedeti veda ca*.

Śruti presents the other *adhikārin* here. *Śruti* is likened to a mother and wants to help the seekers. She is not interested in making a judgement about anybody. She also does not think that anybody is incapable of knowing. But at a given point of time, if the person is not able to understand, then that person has to gain the preparedness in order to know. But that itself is not the means for *mokṣa*. Knowledge alone is the means for *mokṣa* and the knowledge takes place through *śāstra-pramāṇa*. Therefore, for the *pramāṇa* to work, one requires certain preparedness, and the preparedness here is only maturity.

Maturity does not imply absence of any emotional pain. Anybody can have emotional pain, because, that has something to do with the childhood. Maturity is one's understanding, one's non-condemning disposition. One neither condemns oneself, nor does one condemn anybody else; that is all the maturity is about. The unconscious, born of childhood, is a parallel reality that can release certain pain, especially when one grows into a secure person. When one is exposed to the teaching, cognitively one is able to see the teaching clearly. At this time, the unconscious will come out, but that is not in any way opposed to one's maturity or one's knowing. However, it will deny you the fruits of the knowledge, naturally. The unconscious is not a stumbling block but, rather, trying to get out of one's system.

A pain that gets out of the system surfaces as pain before it leaves. Bhagavān covered the unconscious in order to help the child survive, and now, in order to make you not separate from him in any way, Bhagavān just releases it. Therefore, it is not correct to judge oneself by looking at oneself through some pain and saying, 'I am not an *adhikārin* for self-knowledge.' That is not an objective estimation of oneself.

What is necessary is compassion that encompasses all the other qualities mentioned in the *śāstra*. With one's *antaḥkaraṇa* one should be able to accommodate the universe objectively. A commodious heart alone can understand infinite Brahman. We are dealing with the infinite. If a person is compassionate and does not manipulate people, the world, etc., and lives day by day, indeed, he or she is the prepared person.

Living day-by-day is sanity. Live for the day. That is the reality and that is sanity. Just live the day thoroughly, and be alive to what is happening. I have 'today' and I live. There is no morrow. If at all Bhagavān, in the form of one's own *karma,* has a plan for the morrow let him unfold it. One should have that kind of a happy resignation, not the resignation one is driven to, in an inevitable situation. In the awareness of the reality of what is going on, one grows into maturity. That is the real adulthood of a human being. That growth seems to be the only criterion for gaining this *jñāna.*

Acumen is, of course, involved in it because one has to see a fallacious argument as fallacious, at least when it is pointed out. That alone is called a capacity to inquire, to do *vicāra*. That is assumed to be there by the time a person comes to study the *upaniṣad*. In some places, that is not assumed and it is expressly stated.

When we use words such as '*viveka,*' '*vairāgya,*' and the values, we are talking nothing but objectivity and maturity. One has to be very alert with reference to them. They are not less important. We act as though we have them and grow into them. This is the growth. There are areas within myself, perhaps, that I am not even alive to. So those things will come up in life, especially when I am in a spiritual pursuit. As they surface, I can see the shadowed areas and, thus, my whole inner life is like daylight.

A very well lighted *antaḥkaraṇa* is what is said here as maturity. That is also a part of *upaniṣad,* in a way. When *jñāna*, as the means for *mokṣa*, is being talked about, then certain preparedness for that *jñāna* needs to be talked about, if there is a necessity for it; that is the *rahasya.* Why does *mokṣa* not take place for some people, even if they are exposed to the *pramāṇa*?

There is a *rahasya,* a secret here—one must have the preparedness for this knowledge. That is a thing to be said in the *upaniṣad*.

The intention of the *upaniṣad* is not to present a dull student, but to present the difference between *jñāna* and *jñāna-upāya*s, factors that aid knowledge. There are no parallel paths for *mokṣa.*

Here, the *upaniṣad,* with all kindness and compassion—without making any judgement about anybody, without dismissing the student—concludes the teaching. It also concludes to say a few things so that the student can prepare himself or herself. It does not take place overnight. If one wants to become an engineer, overnight one does not become one. One has to work for it; prepare oneself for it. That is how the whole life is.

Mantra 8

तस्यै[83] तपो दमः कर्मेति प्रतिष्ठा। वेदाः सर्वाङ्गानि सत्यमायतनम् ॥ ४.८ ॥

tasyai tapo damaḥ karmeti pratiṣṭhā, vedāḥ sarvāṅgāni satyam āyatanam. (4.8)

tasyai – for that (knowledge of Brahman); *tapaḥ* – self-discipline; *damaḥ* – restraint over senses;

83 तस्यै इति छान्दसप्रयोगः। तस्याः इत्यर्थः।

karma – performance of duty; *iti* – these (are); *pratiṣṭhā* – the support; *vedāḥ* – the four Vedas (are); *sarvāṅgāni* – all the limbs; *satyam* – the truth; *āyatanam* – (is the) abode

Self-discipline, restraint over the senses and performance of (one's) duty are the support for that (knowledge of Brahman). The four Vedas are all the limbs (of it). Truth is (its) abode.

Here the *śāstra* gives a programme of conscious living—being conscious to what one is doing, what one is saying, and what one is thinking—in one's day to day life. This is all about the qualifications required for this knowledge. Let us look into some of these words—*karma, dama, tapas.*

Karma is one's daily prayer.[84] It includes *nitya-karmas*, *karmas* to be performed daily, or regularly at certain intervals, and *naimittika-karmas*—*karmas* that are to be performed on occasions. Being in the family, one has certain responsibilities—daily and occasional. One does all of them properly, living a prayerful life. What is important in *karma* is one's relating to Īśvara. One's daily prayer is not just a routine; it is something alive. One lives one's life of prayer; special prayers helps one accomplish this prayerful life.

---

84 Refer to Pujya Swamiji's book on 'Prayer Guide'.

Dama is just being together, not allowing oneself to be completely dissipated in unproductive pursuits. One can engage in pursuits that are meaningful, that are productive in terms of money, and so on. When meaningless activities are gone from one's life, there is *dama*. *Dama*, here, also stands for *śama*, resolution of the mind.

All that one requires is a simple, prayerful religious life. An irreligious spiritual life does not exist. There is no secular *karma-yoga*. Even for *jijñāsā*, desire for self-knowledge, a religious life is necessary.[85] Religious life means *dharma* and *dharma* means one does not succumb to the pressure of *rāga* and *dveṣa* to go against *dharma*. The word *iti* after the word *karma* means *evam*, which brings in related qualities necessary for self-knowledge. Śaṅkara interprets *iti*[86] as *amānitvādi-guṇas*, virtues like absence of demand for respect, and so on, which are listed in detail in the *Bhagavad Gītā* Chapter XIII.[87]

---

85 *yajñena dānena tapasā anāśakena brāhmaṇāḥ vividiṣanti* (*Bṛhadāraṇyaka Upaniṣad* 4.4.22)

86 इतिशब्दः उपलक्षणत्वप्रदर्शनार्थः। इति एवमाद्यन्दपि ज्ञानोत्पत्तेरुपकारकम् अमानित्वमदम्भित्वम् इत्याद्युपदर्शितं भवति। (केन भाष्यम्)

The word '*iti*' is meant to bring in related qualities. By the word '*iti*' other similar qualifications that are helpful for the knowledge to take place like *amānitvam, adambhitvam* and so on are pointed out.

87 *amānitvam adambhitvam ahiṁsā kṣāntirārjavam, ācāryopāsanaṁ śaucaṁ sthairyam ātmavinigrahaḥ... adhyātma-jñāna-nityatvaṁ tattvajñānārthadarśanam...* (13.7 to 13.11)

Any religious discipline is *tapas*. It is always chosen to address individual's requirement. There are varieties of *tapas.* It includes even the various regimens that we set for ourselves, and then we live up to for achieving the preparedness for self-knowledge.

If *karma, dama* and *tapas* are there, then *brahma-vidyā* is possible. It is said, *brahma-vidyā* should develop feet to stand upon. The *antaḥkaraṇa* is its feet, because knowledge takes place in the *antaḥkaraṇa* alone. Therefore, it should have all the qualifications mentioned in the *śāstra* represented by *karma, dama* and *tapas*. They are like the feet, *pādau iva pādau*. It is said so because all these qualifications are the means by which we understand the *vastu*. One with the mind embellished with these attitudes is capable of gaining the *vidyā*.

If the whole Veda is considered as a person, then Vedanta becomes the *veda-śiras,* the head of the Veda. Then, the *karma-kāṇḍa and upāsanā kāṇḍa* of the Veda are other limbs that support and serve this body, *vedāḥ sarvāṅgāni*. *Satyaṃ āyatanam*: Truth is the abode. *Satya* is *yathārtha-bhāṣaṇam,* speaking the truth. *Satya* is separately mentioned here because the *śāstra* wants to highlight the value of speaking the truth, which stands for all other values. *Āyatana* means the ground on which this body is standing. *Satya* is the ground where the whole Veda-body is standing.

The word, '*satya*' can be taken as the *vastu* also. Since the word '*iti*' coming after the word *karma* covers all other qualities, naturally *satya* also is included in it. Therefore, *satya* can mean the *vastu*. The whole *brahma-vidyā* is standing on the truth that is not subject to negation. For any value, *satya* is *āyatanam*. The whole creation is sustained by that *brahma-vastu* alone. This is the *upaniṣad-rahasya*.

Another *rahasya* is also there. There seems to be no connection between doing one's daily chores—like cooking, walking, sending the children to the school, etc.—and *brahma-vidyā*. Scriptural study alone seems to be directly connected to *brahma-vidyā*. Arjuna also could not see any connection between his fighting the war and *mokṣa* which he wanted. The connection, being not seen, becomes a *rahasya* here.

The various rituals are, sometimes, called *upaniṣad*. We do not know that a particular ritual like *putra-kāmeṣṭi*, for instance, is the means for getting a particular result of begetting a son. Therefore, the connection between a ritual and its result is also *upaniṣad*, a secret. Similarly, living a life of a *karma-yoga* may look unconnected to *mokṣa*, but it does have connection, and the *śāstra* tells us that.

One has to live one's life, assimilate one's experiences and then grow into a complete human being who is qualified for this knowledge.

The natural growth has already taken place at the physical level; no more physical growth is involved. If at all there is growth, it is only inner growth. It is in the hands of the person, in the initiative of the person. One has to usher in that kind of a growth. That is called the *puruṣārtha-niścaya,* ascertainment of *mokṣa* as the goal, or at least *dharma,* for the time being.

Dharma is the means for inner growth. Keeping *mokṣa* as the ultimate goal, then one grows. If *mokṣa* is not kept in view at all, one's growth is going to be stunted and stifled by one's own anxieties, and *rāga-dveṣa*s. If *mokṣa* is kept in view, then everything else easily subserves this main view. If what is at stake is very big, then small things remain small. So, there is a connection between *mokṣa* and our normal daily life. Living one's life in a certain way, with certain attitudes, shows one's completeness and maturity as a human being. That paves the way for one to discover absolute completeness. The *upaniṣad* wanted to give this connection, which is a secret, and created a context through the student's request.

By mentioning the disciple's request, the *śruti* points out that mere *śravaṇa,* even though is the means of knowledge, does not work because one has to prepare oneself. Therefore, the first statement of the teacher is—*upaniṣad* is already taught by me; that is complete. The subsequent statement is—I will tell you now some secret which is also called *upaniṣad,* and which is connected to *brahma-vidyā,* following which you will have a mind conducive to gain the knowledge.

The disciple's question is very important here to remove the separation between knowledge and the means of preparing for knowledge. There are two things here: *jñānasya sādhanam,* and *jñānāya sādhanam.* For gaining knowledge one requires a certain mind, and for that, *karma, dama* and *tapas* are the means; this is *jñānāya sādhanam.* Then *jñānasya sādhanam* is the *pramāṇa.* In other words, *śravaṇa-manana-nididhyāsana* becomes *sākṣāt sādhanam,* the direct means. Here too, *śravaṇa* becomes the direct means for knowledge, with *manana* and *nididhyāsana* as the supporting means. *Śravaṇa* is the *aṅgi,* the primary means, and it becomes effective, efficacious with the support of the secondary means—*manana* and *nididhyāsana.*

Having said this, the *upaniṣad* concludes by mentioning the result of knowledge. That itself conveys a message.

Mantra 9

यो वा एतामेवं वेदापहत्य पाप्मानमनन्ते स्वर्गे लोके
ज्येये प्रतितिष्ठति प्रतितिष्ठति ॥ ४.९ ॥

yo vā etām evaṁ vedāpahatya pāpmānam anante
svarge loke jyeye pratitiṣṭhati pratitiṣṭhati. (4.9)

> *yaḥ* – (that person) who; *vai* – indeed; *etām* –this (*upaniṣad*); *evam* – in this manner; *veda* – knows; *apahatya* – having destroyed; *pāpmānam* – (all) *pāpas*; *anante* – in that which is limitless; *svarge loke* – in the world of *svarga*; *jyeye* – which is the highest; *pratitiṣṭhati* – gets established; *pratitiṣṭhati* – gets established

> Any one who gains the knowledge of Brahman in this manner, having destroyed all *pāpas*, gets established in the limitless and the highest *svarga* (that is Brahman).

Yaḥ, the one (who wants *mokṣa*). *Vai*, whose meaning 'indeed' in the context here points out the one who has prepared oneself for gaining this knowledge by acquiring the necessary qualifications mentioned in the previous *mantra*.

Such a person, *etāṁ brahmavidyām evaṁ veda*, who has this knowledge of Brahman that was pointed out before as *śrotrasya śrotram*, *pratibodha-viditaṁ matam*, and so on, *saḥ pāpmānam apahatya anante svarge loke jyeye pratitiṣṭhati*—being free from *pāpas*, he remains in the limitless Brahman, the highest heaven. The *pāpa* here is *avidyā*, taking oneself to be a *saṁsārin*, which includes its cause, ignorance also. *Avidyā* is used both in the sense of error and the cause for the error. You are *satyaṁ jñānam anantaṁ brahma* in which there is no ignorance. But when you look upon yourself as the doer of actions, the experiencer of the fruits of those actions, and therefore, subject to *puṇya-pāpa*; well, that is due to *avidyā*. Therefore, the error is also called *avidyā.*

The locus of error has to be the object of ignorance also. The locus of the error as well as the locus of ignorance is *ātman*. The product of *avidyā* is that I take myself to be the doer; that is the *pāpa* here. If I eliminate this notion, then I am free. *Pāpa* here also includes *puṇya*.

Negating all the *pāpas*, one remains in *svarga*, heaven. Any heaven is *anitya,* time-bound; therefore, going to *svarga* is not *mokṣa*. There is an adjective *ananta* to the word *svarga. Anante svarge* means in a heaven that does not come to an end.

Then why does the *śāstra* use the word, '*svarga*'? People in general are heaven-bound. There is a message conveyed here that *svarga* is not *mokṣa. Svarga* is an end all right, but that is not the ultimate. Whatever the person is going after, we use a word to refer to that end, and then say that it is not real. If one is after happiness, then we say that it is not the real happiness. We have to use the same word, but then add one adjective 'real'. *Ananta-svarga* is the real heaven. The limitation of *svarga* is removed by saying *anante svarge.*

Ananta means that which is not limited. The word, *svarga* itself means *sukha,* happiness. That is why *svarga* is called *nākam*. *Kam* means *sukha,* pleasure, joy, or happiness. *Akam* means that which is opposed to *sukha*;

that is *duḥkha*. When one more negative prefix is added to *akam*, it becomes *nākam.*[87] The word then means a place where there is no pronounced *duḥkha*, or where there is consistent *sukha,* though there are gradations. Therefore, everybody wants to go to *svarga*. Here, what is talked about is *ananta svarga,* that which is the very source of *sukha,* where *sukha* does not come and go. It is *sukha* in the form of limitlessness in terms of time and degrees.

One wants to be always happy, everywhere and in all situations. That means one has to be of the nature of happiness; only then is it possible. One is not an event, muchless *mokṣa*. So here, *svarga* is referring to the self that is full and complete. In that, the knower of Brahman gets established.

There is another adjective *jyeye.* It means that which is the biggest, that which cannot be improved upon. There is nothing bigger than that. This is Brahman because there is nothing bigger than *brahma*. The word *brahma* itself has that meaning. So *jyeye* means *brahmaṇi,* in Brahman. *Svarge* means in the inner self that is of the nature of *sukha. Sukha* is always for you, a conscious being. When you mention *sukha*, *ātman* is already reckoned. The one who has gained

---

[87] *Akaṁ duḥkhaṁ na vidyāte yasmin* – where there is no *duḥkha,* pain (for the period one is there, there is no disease, old age, etc.)

this *vidyā* is, therefore, no longer the limited self, but Brahman which is non-different from the self.

The word, '*pratitiṣṭhati*' points out that there is no way of getting out of it. It is not some kind of sleep or *samādhi* that one gets into and slip out of. One is Brahman, and therefore, there is no getting out of Brahman. Ignorance does not stage a come back. That means one is no longer separate from Īśvara.

The word, '*pratitiṣṭhati*' is repeated to indicate the conclusion of this dialogue. The text comes down orally. The repetition of the last line or the last word indicates the completion of a particular text. That is the tradition.

Conclusion

Now one can see the whole development in the teaching of the *upaniṣad* very clearly. It started with a question, *keneṣitaṁ patati preṣitaṁ manaḥ iti.* The *śruti* introduced two types of cause by the words, *iṣitam* and *preṣitam*. One cause is that in whose presence a thought, the senses, the *prāṇa* and so on, have their existence. That is the invariable *caitanya*, in which everything has its being. In its presence the mind and the senses become conscious. The existence and consciousness, the *sat* and the *cit*, are lent to everything about yourself. This is one kind of a cause.

The other cause is the very consciousness is in the form of Īśvara, the order. All glories belong to the same Brahman as Īśvara. Therefore, it manifests in various forms. Consciousness alone is Īśvara. Naturally there is no other Īśvara, except you. It is not other than you. But due to the difference of *upādhi*, one is Īśvara, who is all-knowledge, and the other is you, the *jīva*, with limited knowledge. Looking at your mind, senses and body, you make this difference. But the *vastu* is only one Brahman.

This does not in any way negate the presence of differences between the *jīva* and Īśvara. The difference is accepted by the *śāstra* by giving a story. The *deva*s gained victory in a battle with *asura*s, and assumed that the victory was due to their own glories.

They did not recognise Īśvara who made the victory possible. Īśvara taught them the truth. We understand from the story that the *deva*s are there, as individual entities, but the glory belongs to Īśvara. If the *deva*s recognise that, then they are not separate from Īśvara. This recognition is necessary for understanding the oneness between the *jīva* and Īśvara. Teaching *upāsanā* as a means the teacher said, *tadvanaṁ nāma upāsitavyam*—may you therefore meditate upon the presence of Īśvara as one who is in the form of order and glory. To recognise the presence of the Lord is to recognise the glory. That removes the separation from Īśvara to a great extent. Such a person is a real devotee.

In Vedanta you have to go for things that are very real, that keeps this ego under check. There are two types of *sādhana* in Vedanta. One is listening to the *śāstra* and the other is your relating to Īśvara. Everything else will create a bloated ego, one that is more oriented to the body. If *yoga* is taken as a discipline meant for *mokṣa, yoga* also is Īśvara's glory. If you recognise Īśvara's glory in every *āsana* then there is spiritual *sādhana*, there is devotion.

Without devotion, without connecting to Īśvara, anything you do is not going to help spiritually. Lord Kṛṣṇa says throughout the *Gītā*, "Do not at any time get away from me." You need to recognise the glory of Īśvara—in your life, in others' lives, in the creation. The more you recognise glories of Īśvara you are allowing Īśvara to manifest through you. This is what the *śruti* teaches in *tadvanaṁ nāma upāsitavyam.*

After looking into the *upaniṣads,* I find that an act of devotion, prayer, *pūjā* and so on, become more real as we get more insight. Your account has to be settled with Īśvara. The more we look into it, the more we find that a religious life alone would help us grow and discover what is.

ॐ आप्यायन्तु ममाङ्गानि वाक्प्राणश्चक्षुः श्रोत्रमथो बलमिन्द्रियाणि च सर्वाणि । सर्वं ब्रह्मौपनिषदम् । माहं ब्रह्म निराकुर्यां मा मा ब्रह्म निराकरोत् । अनिराकरणमस्त्वनिराकरणं मेऽस्तु । तदात्मनि निरते य उपनिषत्सु धर्मास्ते मयि सन्तु । ते मयि सन्तु ॥ ॐ शान्तिः शान्तिः शान्तिः

केनोपनिषत् समाप्ता

Kenopaniṣad is complete

Oṁ tat sat

Kenopaniṣad Text

केनोपनिषत् पाठः

शान्तिपाठः

ॐ आप्यायन्तु ममाङ्गानि वाक्प्राणश्चक्षुः श्रोत्रमथो बलमिन्द्रियाणि च सर्वाणि । सर्वं ब्रह्मौपनिषदम् । माहं ब्रह्म निराकुर्याम् । मा मा ब्रह्म निराकरोत् । अनिराकरणमस्त्वनिराकरणं मेऽस्तु । तदात्मनि निरते य उपनिषत्सु धर्मास्ते मयि सन्तु । ते मयि सन्तु ॥ ॐ शान्तिः शान्तिः शान्तिः ॥

खण्ड १

ॐ केनेषितं पतति प्रेषितं मनः
केन प्राणः प्रथमः प्रैति युक्तः ।
केनेषितां वाचमिमां वदन्ति
चक्षुः श्रोत्रं क उ देवो युनक्ति ॥ १.१ ॥

श्रोत्रस्य श्रोत्रं मनसो मनो यत्
वाचो ह वाचं स उ प्राणस्य प्राणः ।
चक्षुषश्चक्षुरतिमुच्य धीराः
प्रेत्यास्माल्लोकादमृता भवन्ति ॥ १.२ ॥

न तत्र चक्षुर्गच्छति न वाग्गच्छति नो मनो
न विद्मो न विजानीमो यथैतदनुशिष्यात्।
अन्यदेव तद्विदितादथो अविदितादधि
इति शुश्रुम पूर्वेषां ये नस्तद्व्याचचक्षिरे ॥ १.३ ॥

यद्वाचानभ्युदितं येन वागभ्युद्यते।
तदेव ब्रह्म त्वं विद्धि नेदं यदिदमुपासते ॥ १.४ ॥

यन्मनसा न मनुते येनाहुर्मनो मतम्।
तदेव ब्रह्म त्वं विद्धि नेदं यदिदमुपासते ॥ १.५ ॥

यच्चक्षुषा न पश्यति येन चक्षूꣳषि पश्यति।
तदेव ब्रह्म त्वं विद्धि नेदं यदिदमुपासते ॥ १.६ ॥

यच्छ्रोत्रेण न शृणोति येन श्रोत्रमिदꣳश्रुतम्।
तदेव ब्रह्म त्वं विद्धि नेदं यदिदमुपासते ॥ १.७ ॥

यत्प्राणेन न प्राणिति येन प्राणः प्रणीयते।
तदेव ब्रह्म त्वं विद्धि नेदं यदिदमुपासते ॥ १.८ ॥

खण्ड २

यदि मन्यसे सुवेदेति दहरमेवापि[1]
नूनं त्वं वेत्थ ब्रह्मणो रूपम्।
यदस्य त्वं यदस्य देवेष्वथ नु मीमाꣳस्यमेव ते।
मन्ये विदितम्॥ २.१॥

नाहं मन्ये सुवेदेति नो न वेदेति वेद च।
यो नस्तद्वेद तद्वेद नो न वेदेति वेद च॥ २.२॥

यस्यामतं तस्य मतं मतं यस्य न वेद सः।
अविज्ञातं विजानतां विज्ञातमविजानताम्॥ २.३॥

प्रतिबोधविदितं मतममृतत्वं हि विन्दते।
आत्मना विन्दते वीर्यं विद्यया विन्दतेऽमृतम्॥ २.४॥

इह चेदवेदीदथ सत्यमस्ति न चेदिहावेदीन्महती विनष्टिः।
भूतेषु भूतेषु विचित्य धीराः प्रेत्यास्माल्लोकादमृता भवन्ति॥ २.५॥

खण्ड ३

ब्रह्म ह देवेभ्यो विजिग्ये। तस्य ह ब्रह्मणो विजये देवा अमहीयन्त॥ ३.१॥

त ऐक्षन्त। अस्माकमेवायं विजयोऽस्माकमेवायं
महिमेति। तद्धैषां विजज्ञौ। तेभ्यो ह प्रादुर्बभूव।
तन्न व्यजानत किमिदं यक्षमिति॥ ३.२॥

तेऽग्निमब्रुवञ्जातवेद एतद्विजानीहि किमिदं
यक्षमिति। तथेति॥ ३.३॥

तदभ्यद्रवत्तमभ्यवदत्कोऽसीत्यग्निर्वा
अहमस्मीत्यब्रवीज्जातवेदा वा अहमस्मीति॥३.४॥

तस्मिꣳस्त्वयि किं वीर्यमिति। अपीदꣳसर्वं दहेयं
यदिदं पृथिव्यामिति ॥ ३.५॥

तस्मै तृणं निदधावेतद्दहेति। तदुपप्रेयाय
सर्वजवेन। तन्न शशाक दग्धुम्।
स तत एव निववृते। नैतदशकं विज्ञातुं
यदेतद्यक्षमिति॥ ३.६॥

अथ वायुमब्रुवन्। वायवेतद्विजानीहि
किमेतद्यक्षमिति। तथेति॥ ३.७॥

दभ्यद्रवत्तमभ्यवदत्कोऽसीति। वायुर्वा
अहमस्मीत्यब्रवीन्मातरिश्वा वा अहमस्मीति॥३.८॥

तस्मिꣳस्त्वयि किं वीर्यमित्यपीदꣳसर्वमाददीय यदिदं पृथिव्यामिति ॥ ३.९ ॥

तस्मै तृणं निदधावेतदादत्स्वेति। तदुपप्रेयाय सर्वजवेन। तन्न शशाकादातुम्। स तत एव निववृते। नैतदशकं विज्ञातुं यदेतद्यक्षमिति ॥ ३.१० ॥

अथेन्द्रमब्रुवन्मघवन्नेतद्विजानीहि किमेतद्यक्षमिति। तथेति। तदभ्यद्रवत्तस्मात्तिरोदधे ॥ ३. ११ ॥

स तस्मिन्नेवाकाशे स्त्रियमाजगाम बहुशोभमानामुमाꣳहैमवतीम्। ताꣳहोवाच किमेतद्यक्षमिति ॥ ३.१२ ॥

खण्ड ४

सा ब्रह्मेति होवाच। ब्रह्मणो वा एतद्विजये महीयध्वमिति। ततो हैव विदाञ्चकार ब्रह्मेति ॥ ४.१ ॥

तस्माद्वा एते देवा अतितरामिवान्यान्देवान् यदग्निर्वायुरिन्द्रः। ते ह्येनन्नेदिष्ठं पस्पृशुः। ते ह्येनत्प्रथमो विदाञ्चकार ब्रह्मेति ॥ ४.२ ॥

तस्माद्वा इन्द्रोऽतितरामिव अन्यान्देवान्। स ह्येनन्नेदिष्ठं पस्पर्श। स ह्येनत्प्रथमो विदाञ्चकार ब्रह्मेति॥ ४.३॥

तस्यैष आदेशो यदेतद्विद्युतो व्यद्युतदा ३ इतीन्न्यमीमिषदा ३ इत्यधिदैवतम्॥ ४.४॥

अथाध्यात्मम्। यदेतद्गच्छतीव च मनोऽनेन चैतदुपस्मरत्यभीक्ष्णꣳसङ्कल्पः॥ ४.५॥

तद्ध तद्वनं नाम। तद्वनमित्युपासितव्यम्। स य एतदेवं वेदाभि हैनꣳसर्वाणि भूतानि संवाञ्छन्ति॥४.६॥

उपनिषदं भो ब्रूहीत्युक्ता त उपनिषद्ब्राह्मी वाव त उपनिषदमब्रूमेति॥ ४.७॥

तस्यै तपो दमः कर्मेति प्रतिष्ठा वेदाः सर्वाङ्गानि सत्यमायतनम्॥ ४.८॥

यो वा एतामेवं वेदापहत्य पाप्मानमनन्ते स्वर्गे लोके ज्येये प्रतितिष्ठति प्रतितिष्ठति॥ ४.९॥

॥ इति केनोपनिषत् समाप्ता॥

Alphabetical Index to Mantras

Books by Swami Dayananda Saraswati

Public Talk Series :

1. Living Intelligently
2. Successful Living
3. Need for Cognitive Change
4. Discovering Love
5. Value of Values
6. Vedic View and Way of Life

Upaniṣad Series :

7. Muṇḍakopaniṣad
8. Kenopaniṣad

Text Translation Series :

9. Śrīmad Bhagavad Gītā

   (Text with roman transliteration and English translation)

10. Śrī Rudram

    (Text in Sanskrit with transliteration, word-to-word and verse meaning along with an elaborate commentary in English)

Stotra Series :

11. Dipārādhanā
12. Prayer Guide

    (With explanations of several Mantras, Stotras, Kirtans and Religious Festivals)

Moments with Oneself Series :

13. Freedom from Helplessness
14. Living versus Getting On
15. Insights
16. Action and Reaction
17. Fundamental Problem
18. Problem is You, Solution is You
19. Purpose of Prayer
20. Vedanta 24x7
21. Freedom
22. Crisis Management
23. Surrender and Freedom
24. The Need for Personal Reorganisation
25. Freedom in Relationship
26. Stress-free Living
27. Om Namo Bhagavate Vāsudevāya
28. Yoga of Objectivity

Bhagavad Gītā Series :

29. Bhagavad Gītā Home Study Program (Hardbound) *

Meditation Series :

30. Morning Meditation Prayers

* Under print in new format

Essays :

31. Do all Religions have the same goal?
32. Conversion is Violence
33. Gurupūrṇimā
34. Dānam
35. Japa
36. Can We?
37. Moments with Krishna
38. **Teaching Tradition of Advaita Vedanta**

Exploring Vedanta Series : (*vākyavicāra*)

39. śraddhā bhakti dhyāna yogād avaihi ātmānaṁ ced vijānīyāt

Books by Pujya Swamiji's disciples :

Sadhvi Varadaa Caitanya

40. Bhagavad Gītā Home Study Program

    (Hardbound) Kannada translation based on the original Gītā Home Study Program—English.3 Volumes available.

Dr. Carol Whitfield

41. The Jungian Myth and Advaita Vedanta
42. The Vedantic Self and the Jungian Psyche

Books by Smt. Sheela Balaji :

43. Salutations to Rudra
    (based on the exposition of Śrī Rudram by Swami Dayananda Saraswati)
44. Without a Second

Also available at :

ARSHA VIDYA RESEARCH
AND PUBLICATION TRUST
32/4 Sir Desika Road
Mylapore Chennai 600 004
Telefax : 044 - 2499 7131
Email : avrandpc@gmail.com

ARSHA VIDYA GURUKULAM
Anaikatti P.O.
Coimbatore 641 108
Ph : 0422 - 2657001
Fax : 0422 - 2657002
Email : office@arshavidya.in

ARSHA VIDYA GURUKULAM
P.O.Box 1059. Pennsylvania
PA 18353, USA.
Ph : 001-570-992-2339
Email : avp@epix.net

SWAMI DAYANANDA ASHRAM
Purani Jhadi, P.B. No. 30
Rishikesh, Uttaranchal 249 201
Telefax : 0135-2430769
Email : ashrambookstore@yahoo.com

AND IN ALL THE LEADING BOOK STORES, INDIA